Interior Solutions
from Armstrong™

the 1960s

C. Eugene Moore

4880 Lower Valley Road, Atglen, PA 19310 USA

Dedication

With love for each of them, this book is dedicated to Emily, Kevin, Kelly, and Scott Moore—because the sun beams brightly in any room they happen to occupy.

Library of Congress Cataloging-in-Publication Data

Moore, C. Eugene, 1931-
    Interior solutions from Armstrong the 1960s/C. Eugene
    Moore.
       p. cm.
    ISBN 0-7643-0700-2 (pbk.)
    1. Armstrong World Industries. 2. Interior decoration--United
States--History--20th century-Themes, motives. I. title.
NK2004.3.A74M664   1999
747.2'0496--dc21   98-46031
                       CIP

Designed by "Sue"
Type set in Dom Bold BT/Humanist 521 BT

ISBN: 0-7643-0700-2
Printed in China

Published by Schiffer Publishing Ltd.
4880 Lower Valley Road
Atglen, PA 19310
Phone: (610) 593-1777; Fax: (610) 593-2002
E-mail: Schifferbk@aol.com
Please visit our web site catalog at **www.schifferbooks.com**

This book may be purchased from the publisher.
Include $3.95 for shipping.
Please try your bookstore first.
We are interested in hearing from authors
with book ideas on related subjects.
You may write for a free catalog.

In Europe, Schiffer books are distributed by
Bushwood Books
6 Marksbury Rd.
Kew Gardens
Surrey TW9 4JF England
Phone: 44 (0)181 392-8585; Fax: 44 (0)181 392-9876
E-mail: Bushwd@aol.com

Contents

Penthouse apartment with a view, inside and out. See page 170.

Acknowledgments

All the illustrations of room interiors included in this book are the property of Armstrong World Industries, Inc. (or, as it was known at the time the rooms were created, Armstrong Cork Company). I'm grateful to the company for allowing me access to them, for without such cooperation the book would not have been possible.

My hope is that the people at Armstrong will find a satisfying reward as they review these ten years' worth of truly magnificent interiors. They should, for the rooms certainly reflect great credit on the company.

Several Armstrong employees deserve recognition for the help they provided during the course of writing and reviewing the book. They include Douglas E. Winters, David D. Wilson, and Jane Reidenbach. I thank them for their assistance.

Rose M. Fronczak, keeper of Armstrong's archives, has earned her own private paragraph on this page because she has played such a special part in the preparation of this book on the 1960s. Not only did she unlock the company's archival mysteries but also she came up with suggestions on source materials that would prove invaluable to me. Rose is always full of ideas, and in my experience every one she ever had has been a good one.

Though I did not find it possible to identify the specific designer or team of designers for each room included here, it is important to recognize the creativity of Armstrong's interior designers through the years. Their work is unmatched, anywhere. I trust that those whose room interiors are included share with me the feeling that this book serves a valuable purpose if it helps to preserve the beauty and practicality they have produced, so further generations may enjoy them.

Perhaps it seems odd to include the publisher's name in the acknowledgments. But in fact the people at Schiffer Publishing Ltd. have proven a joy to work with, throughout this long journey. I'm speaking notably of Peter Schiffer, Douglas Congdon-Martin, Bruce Waters, and Blair Loughrey. And did you suppose for even a moment that I've forgotten Nancy Schiffer? Unlikely! Her suggestions were, as always, solid and meaningful. But what she really provided was encouragement. Cheerful, never-flagging encouragement. That meant more than I can express.

Most of all, I wish to acknowledge the steady presence of my wife, Jan. She worked alongside me all along the way, and to the extent this book is successful she deserves the major credit.

To all these people, my sincere thanks.

Introduction

The 1960s were different.

Oh, there was no climactic, going-over-the-waterfall event that ushered in the new decade as the clock struck midnight. It was more subtle than that. Historical events don't generally check the calendar. Whether they occur gradually or with cataclysmic force, they take place at times of their own choosing.

But in the context of history, the '60s were something special. Even some of the changes that were slow in developing would have prolonged effects. Consider the civil rights movement and the environmental movement, both of which pulled themselves together during this decade. Consider the war in Viet Nam, which would claim 57,000 American lives and whose scars would still ache and burn years afterward. Consider the birth control pill, which attained widespread use during the 1960s across a world that would never be quite the same.

It was a time of shocking tragedy, our headlines splashed with the bloodstains of three assassinations: John F. Kennedy, Martin Luther King, Jr., Robert Kennedy. It was the decade in which concrete and barbed wire came to symbolize man's inability to get along with even his closest neighbors, as during one despairingly dark night a wall went up to separate East Berlin from West Berlin.

Several years later, history's largest "happening" took place on a 600-acre farm near Bethel, New York. They called it Woodstock, and the thousands of young men and women who took part could no more explain how this event was to become so significant than their parents could. But significant it was.

Other events left their mark on our memories. In the mid-1960s, a jet plane touched down in New York, and the waiting crowd turned even more frenzied. Out stepped the mop-topped group of young men whom America had been waiting for. Would we ever forget the Beatles? Having almost as great an impact on our culture was the introduction of an imaginative new children's program for television, named "Sesame Street."

Almost at the end of the decade occurred an event that would sweep most other news off the front page. At 10:56 p.m. Eastern time on July 20, 1969, Neil Armstrong became the first earthling to set foot on the moon: "That's one small step for man, one giant leap for mankind." And, as the millions who were watching on television agreed, he was right about that.

During this ten-year period of upheaval in culture, politics, and technology, the U.S. economy was quietly, and sometimes not so quietly, making some changes of its own. The 1950s, the first full decade after the end of World War II, was a time of building, of staking out a place for new and growing families, of pulling one's feet under oneself to prepare for the future. It was a good time. The '60s were in many respects even better. Despite occasional downswings in the economy, the nation buttered this period with optimism, almost with swaggering confidence. Jobs were available; and more important, even better jobs lay ahead for those prepared to cope with the technical changes that were flying at us like a barrage of electronic arrows.

Interiors show a new emphasis

At Armstrong, as in the nation as a whole, the decade was one of change. Even the room interiors shown in the company's advertisements were different. From the beginning, Armstrong designers had created rooms that were chock-full of ideas, ideas that home owners could adapt for their own interiors. Such ideas certainly filled the company's ads of the 1950s (see *Inspiring Interiors from Armstrong—the 1950s*, Schiffer Publishing Ltd., 1998). During the 1960s, though, Armstrong ads gradually changed. Now the emphasis was not so much on beautiful, *idea-filled* room interiors as on *beautiful*, idea-filled room interiors. The rooms were still beautiful, and they still were full of ideas. But the balance had shifted.

One reason was that the starter homes built after World War II by veterans clutching G.I. Bill mortgages in their fists were by now being replaced by larger new houses, aimed at accommodating growing families.

Another reason, allied to the first, was the increasing affluence of the American consumer. Families were learning that they could afford homes with more spacious rooms, more conveniences, more luxurious furnishings. This meant, in turn, that Armstrong's interior designers could spread their wings and fluff out their feathers to create room interiors of a type rarely seen before.

Still another reason, and of greatest importance, was the development of new types of flooring. The beginning of the 1950s had been marked mainly by the use of linoleum and asphalt tile; only toward the end of that decade was vinyl flooring coming into prominence. During the 1960s, though, vinyl took over the throne that it still occupies today. These were heady days for Armstrong. Its research, engineering, and manufacturing arms were working together to produce flooring materials with improved wear characteristics and easier installation. Armstrong product designers were creating flooring materials of unparalleled beauty, unlike anything previously seen in the marketplace. Similar advancements were being made in Armstrong ceiling materials. So the company's interior designers were able to turn their imaginations loose as never before, taking advantage of the new product innovations and originating room interiors that would appeal to a broad sweep of consumers.

A new force comes to Armstrong

It's worth noting that the handsome rooms Armstrong designers offered during the 1960s represent the lengthened shadow of someone who had joined the company about 40 years earlier.

Hazel Dell Brown, a Pratt Institute graduate, was supervisor of art education in the Indianapolis school system when Armstrong approached her. At first she demurred. What use would a company that made a basic, almost commodity product such as linoleum have for someone like her? But she was a widow in her late 20s, and she was adventurous enough to try the new opportunity that was being offered to her. In the fall of 1921 she became Armstrong's first interior decorator. In the long history of the company, hardly anyone would have a greater effect on establishing the corporate personality that Armstrong would present to the world.

In high heels, Mrs. Brown stood just over 5 feet tall. She weighed barely 100 pounds. We know this from the employee record she filled out when she began her association with Armstrong. (In those days, companies expected information they would not ask for today. To the question "Do you own your home or rent?" she wrote in "own," though she declined to supply the amount of "the present value of your home.")

Anyone who was fortunate enough to have been around her during her Armstrong career would remember Hazel Dell Brown as an especially active electron—a tiny but dynamic force. Wearing a trademark black velvet bow in her hair, like a hummingbird she would hover over every room her staff designed as it was being readied for photography. Every room had to be more than visually appealing. It also must offer practicality, she insisted, with innovative suggestions that the homemaker and home owner could pick up and make their own. Until she was satisfied, the room was never complete.

She was to become the decorating voice of America. Every day, from across the United States, letters poured in to her as homemakers sought solutions to their decorating problems. And every one of them was answered, sometimes with an enclosed swatch of fabric or a sample of paint, always with a helpful suggestion or two.

In 1957, at age 65, Hazel Dell Brown retired from active service. Fortunately, her sense of artistic perfectionism had been passed along to the talented interior designers who would succeed her at Armstrong.

In this book you will see the results of their efforts. They created interiors of surpassing beauty, interiors from which people today can draw usable ideas, interiors that are too important to be overlooked in the passage of time.

Enjoy reading the book and inspecting the room interiors it contains. And consider how the rooms you meet here can be used to make your own home more attractive, more comfortable, and easier to care for.

—C. Eugene Moore

Hazel Dell Brown

Chapter 1

Kitchens

In many respects the kitchen is the "central heating system" of the home. It's where the family finds its focus. Here gather the cooks, of whatever gender, to begin the process of nourishment, of whatever type. Though it's one of the areas of the home that has a specific, well-defined purpose, its usage broadened during the 1960s as the average size of the kitchen grew. Now it often included an eat-in area and thus became a gathering place for friends. Armstrong showed how it could take on this added function attractively.

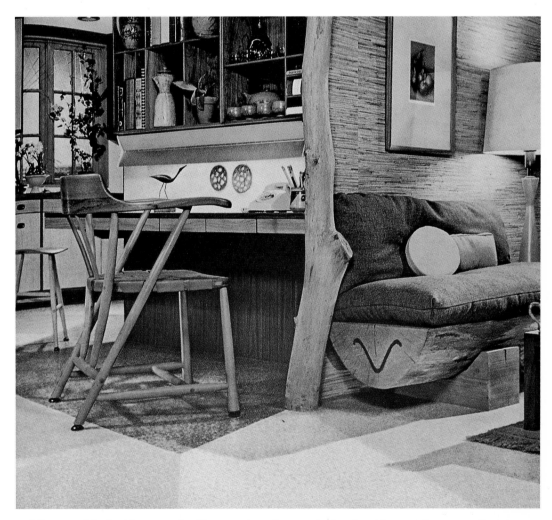

Like a cabin in the woods. Can you imagine preparing food in a setting as rustic as this, and yet with every up-to-date convenience? Natural wood-grains establish a restful, carefree mood in the kitchen at left, with its built-in breakfast bar that doubles as a writing desk. Above are shelves for some of the family's favorite collectibles. At right, just past a divider created from the upright bole of a tree, is the family's activities room. You're right about the sofa: it's made from half a log, with cushions added, set into a heavy wooden base that rests on the floor.

Revitalizing a farm kitchen. What better place to establish an early American theme than the kitchen of an old farmhouse that's being brought up to date? Almost every home has at least some furnishings from days gone by; and if these are cherished family hand-me-downs, so much the better. You can supplement them with items purchased at sales and auctions, such as the churns and antique kitchen utensils in this room. The schoolmarm chairs and braided rug are set off by a linoleum design that resembles wide-plank pegged floors.

Same room, four decorative treatments. Changing the interior design of a room can alter its entire character. Here's the same kitchen wearing four different changes of clothing. In (1) the room is furnished in the Renaissance manner. Individuality is aided by the embossed flagstone appearance of the linoleum. A slight alteration in the cabinet arrangement (2), and the room takes on an entirely different look. The floor design features small pebble-like elements. In (3) the room becomes an up-to-the-minute home work center. The flooring features small-scale tiles. In (4) a glittering starburst pattern in the linoleum turns the kitchen into an exciting place for the family to gather for breakfast.

1

2

3

4

Crowning touch for a kitchen. If you have a ceiling that's cracked or peeling, here's the solution. Install a *new* ceiling right over the old one. In this kitchen, designed to show off a collection of porcelain ware, the new ceiling tile provides more than an attractive overhead surface. It's an acoustical type, so it soaks up noise. And it's designed for installation by the do-it-yourselfer. Back in the 1960s, when this Armstrong ad appeared, a ceiling like the one in this 10' x 12' room cost well under $50, including all materials.

Opposite:
All set to stay spotless. The focal point of this kitchen is the sink area, with its array of potted plants echoing the greenery just outside the window. And just above it is a clever hideaway cabinet that holds often-used items within easy reach. Best of all, the furnishings in the room are designed for easy maintenance. The chairs wipe clean with a damp cloth. The flooring is a sheet type, virtually seamless. Note how it's coved up under the cabinets, so there's no sharp corner to catch dirt.

Like horizontal exclamation points. See how the courageous use of stripes in vivid colors can add an unforgettable verve to an otherwise quiet room. Varied textures are found in the painted brick and in the nubbly surface of the vinyl sheet flooring. With the addition of a home entertainment center, this becomes more than an ordinary kitchen. Now it's a place in which the family is happy to welcome guests. Why, it's even a place to practice the guitar. Did anybody see where I left my plectrum?

Adapted from African origins. Artifacts from other parts of the world present many ideas for unusual decorative themes. This striking kitchen was inspired by the motifs used by some of the people indigenous to Africa. The strongly parallel lines found in the low table and chairs are carried forward by the treatment of cabinets and walls. The bright accents of the floor are there to stay, as they're set right into the vinyl-content tile. It's a type suitable for do-it-yourself installation. An area for relaxing (see inset) adjoins the kitchen.

An eat-in area that's easy to use. Most breakfast bars are counter height. Nothing wrong with that idea, though it does mean that you have to perch on a stool to reach the food. This one was more thoughtfully designed. Its surface is a few inches lower than the counter, so you can sit in comfort on chairs. Lining the breakfast bar are drawers for tableware and napkins. The spindled legs and backs of the chairs are complemented by the tile-like effect in the sheet flooring.

Take another look—it's not what it seems.
The handsome brick and wood floor you see
here isn't brick and isn't wood. It's one of a
collection of sheet flooring materials that look
like the real thing (others resemble flagstone
and Spanish tile) but that offer the advantages
of modern vinyl. In this kitchen and adjoining
dining room (see inset), the brick and wood
textures set off cherished early-twentieth-
century furnishings that include a coffee bin,
painted wooden chairs, and a flower-petal light
fixture. And there's built-in storage space
everywhere you look.

15

Breakfast at the riding club. If your kitchen is to have an eat-in area, with a bit of thought and planning you can set it off from the ordinary. This one draws its inspiration from the stable, with the breakfast nook suggesting a stall. Hanging stirrups serve as conversation-piece napkin rings. In the kitchen portion of the room, gleaming pots and pans are easy to reach when it's time to use them but otherwise add to the decorative whole. The pebbly look of the vinyl sheet flooring goes nicely with the varied textures of wood, leather, and brass.

The kitchen that can't decide whether it's in or out.
It's some of each, really. The inside portion (foreground) features modern appliances, a dining nook with comfortable chairs, a built-in desk, and vinyl-content tile flooring for easy sweep-ups. Outside the sliding doors is the summertime annex, with its barbecue grill and its furniture of wicker and wrought iron. A shelf near the top of the board fence provides a place for a row of potted plants.

A beautiful burst of bouquets. Someone who likes flowers can never have too many of them, and this room seeks to answer the call. It's designed around a collection of half a dozen floral prints, some of which serve as doors to storage cabinets. Potted plants above the sink and on glass shelves near the breakfast nook carry out the flowery theme. Above the built-in desk is a bulletin board for tacking up recipes, small samples of spices, or packets of flower seeds. In the center background, pull-out shelves provide a new, handy way to store canned goods.

Opposite:
Break out the bandannas. Here's a kitchen that, despite its small size, actually looks spacious. One reason for this is the large expanse of windows in the breakfast nook, as they allow sunlight to flood into the kitchen. Another is the clever provision of storage space, so hardly an inch is wasted and there's no need for the clutter found in some kitchens. For example, recipe books are stored beneath the telephone desk. Red bandanna cloth covering the stool is duplicated in the wallpaper and various accessories. The louvered doors on the upper cabinets provide an attractive complement.

A warm breeze from the Mediterranean. The Spanish tile in this kitchen isn't Spanish tile at all. It's a vinyl sheet flooring. Together with the rich woods and the large woven basket, it gives the room an unmistakable aura of southern Europe. To cook appropriate foods in such a setting calls for a variety of spices. Look how that's provided for here, with shelves full of imported types, each in its own labeled container. Surrounding the sink at right is the cook's own herb garden; so adding zest to a meal is just a matter of reaching out one's hand.

Special touches added at low cost. Even if your budget is stretched so tight you can strum it like a zither, you can still find ways to give your home a look that identifies it as your own. In this kitchen, a moderately priced metal dinette table is covered by a fringed cloth and flanked by folding "director's chairs." A vinyl sheet flooring provides practicality in maintenance. In the dining room adjoining, a crenelated cornice at the window adds a note of distinction while harmonizing with the carpet and the natural wood-grain finishes.

Opportunities for above-eye-level appeal. When we consider decorating a room, sometimes we overlook the possibilities that exist at or near the ceiling. But see what has been done here with just a few design elements. On the plate rail, beautiful tableware is set off against a floral border that echoes the strong fabric and wallpaper motifs. Redware mugs add interest at the corner. The ceiling is a type that's especially appropriate for kitchens. It's acoustical, so it absorbs noise, and it's coated with vinyl for easy cleanups.

Sunshine and shadows. Sometimes forgotten is the part that lighting, natural or artificial, can play in a decorative scheme. Here sunlight floods into the kitchen every morning, and the room is designed to take advantage of that. Can you imagine a brighter, more cheerful place to have break- fast? As the sun moves across the sky, even the play of shadows on the sheet flooring adds a changing accent to the whole effect. Reflecting the wickerwork of the chairs are the treatment of the upper cabinets and the mesh weave of the curtains.

You don't have to settle for the ordinary. Kitchen floors have to be practical, but they don't have to be mundane. This one, of a vinyl sheet material in an effect that resembles variegated pebbles, takes its cue from the brick archway of the pass-through. The sweeping curves of the flooring installation help to lighten up the heavy carved doors of the cupboards. The floor is often the largest decorating element in a room, so it makes sense to consider it early when you're planning an interior design.

Inviting the out-of-doors inside. If you like the appearance and texture found in natural materials (who doesn't?), there's no reason you can't enjoy them in the interior of your home. This room suggests ways to make use of stone and wood-grains in an attractive manner. It doesn't sacrifice modern convenience, though. The flooring, for example, is of an easy-to-swish-clean vinyl-content tile. Feature strips of contrasting colors make the kitchen seem wider than it really is. The stools blend nicely with the interior and provide seating at a comfortable height for the counter. The fireplace has a built-in barbecue spit. And the windows "bend" to let in more light.

Swing among the moonbeams. In this kitchen the chairs don't pull up to the table. Instead, the breakfast bar pulls up to the padded basket chairs suspended from the ceiling. Because the bar is on casters, it rolls over to become extra counter space during the time of food preparation. The well-lighted area above the range includes a vented hood to carry away cooking odors. At left is a pull-out storage cupboard for pots and pans, so they're right within reach. By day, the vinyl sheet flooring is bright and cheerful; at night it takes on a deep, pearly glow to add a touch of elegance to entertaining.

Opposite:
Bright as an art exhibit. In fact, this kitchen *is* a work of art, with its emphasis on strong rectangles reminiscent of European geometric painting. But it's a working kitchen, too, designed to make food preparation as enjoyable as possible. The tall, comfortable stools allow you to work at the counter with ease. Utensils and other frequently used items are at eye level, within the cook's easy grasp. Oven mitts and drying towels are kept in a slideaway, hideaway cabinet at the end of the counter so they're out of sight when not needed.

Left:
Weaving a spell—colorful as well. If you want to be delightfully daring in your kitchen design, go ahead. You can come up with something that's truly unforgettable. Here the color starts with the vinyl sheet flooring, then takes off in interesting new directions. Note the napkins tied to the backs of the chairs. And see how light filtering through the latticework contributes to the unusual shadow pictures that form on floor and walls. Daisy designs cut into the cupboard doors provide a freshness that's echoed in the rolling storage unit that houses homemade jams and other foods.

Pardon me, is that a tree in your kitchen? Well, yes, and it makes a wonderful place for hanging lanterns of various designs. The idea may seem offbeat, but don't let it distract you from the practical features that this room is full of. As an illustration, note how pleasantly the vertical paneling is used on the refrigerator and on the lower facing of the island counter. Storage space is bounteous. And all that cabinetry is up and off the floor, where it's easy to clean under. The flooring, too, was selected with maintenance in mind. It's a vinyl sheet material, and a few swipes of a dust mop are all that's usually needed to keep it spotless.

Opposite:

A room to highlight special belongings. As they travel, the people who live in this home love to collect furnishings that catch their eye. Their kitchen has a decided Mediterranean flavor, and each treasured piece has an opportunity to shine. The pierced metal of the chandelier inspired the overhead lights at the sink. The vibrantly colorful floor suggests expensive inlaid tile. But look again. That floor is a vinyl sheet material, with almost no seams to catch the dirt. Even the family dog is provided for, with his own house decoratively tied in to the overall scheme.

Left:

A second chance for an old kitchen. In an older home, the kitchen can become out of date—not only because new appliances and other conveniences are being introduced all the time but also because the room receives so much use. Here's how a kitchen can be given a sprightly new dress without losing any of its appeal. Just installing a new floor, such as this vinyl sheet material, can give the room a lift. In this instance, new furniture and reworked cabinetry also help. The pass-through feature of the brick fireplace enables the library to double as a family room for dinners around the hearth.

Baskets of daisies. If you like to surround yourself with flowers, here's a room that you'd enjoy having in your home. And see how simple it is to create such an interior! The floral wallpaper is applied to the inside of the pull-down curtains to further the theme. And wicker baskets, which go so well with the natural beauty of the flowers, are used at every opportunity. Perishables, for example, are stored in baskets that slide under the counter, so air can circulate around them. The cabinet doors repeat the woven wicker effect.

Opposite:
A kitchen suitable for buffet dining. A blending of calm, cool colors; the contrast of straight lines and geometrics—suddenly, a vivid showplace of a room! In a kitchen as elegant as this, why not use it for guest dinners? The roll-about bar makes serving simple, right from the counter, and clean-ups just as easy. The vertical wood paneling is carried out consistently on appliance facing, walls, and counters, and it's complemented by the geometric tile-like design of the vinyl sheet flooring.

Left:
Stir in the sunshine. When you're following your favorite recipe, work with plenty of light. That's certainly possible in a kitchen like this. The window-wall leading to the porch brings all the natural beauty of the out-of-doors right into the room with you. The room itself is open, uncluttered, and inviting. A dazzling new floor, in a vinyl-content tile, is the base for the entire color scheme. This type of flooring is designed for installation by either do-it-yourselfers or professional installers.

Right for the kitchen: a grease-resistant ceiling. The ceiling here is vinyl-coated to make it resistant to the greasy residue that always seems to build up over time in a kitchen. It can be swiped clean with a damp cloth—or even repainted, if desired. Further, it's a suspended ceiling. That means that the home handyman who installed it was able to lower a too-high ceiling in an older home, at the same time concealing pipes and wiring. And doesn't it make an attractive overhead for this reinvigorated, modern kitchen?

Using kitchen accouterment as decorative accessories. Cutting boards on the wall, gleaming pans under the range hood, even storage containers for cooking staples can become part of the decorative theme when they're chosen with care. The main elements of this homey room were selected with maintenance in mind. The flooring, for example, is a vinyl sheet type that comes in 12-foot widths. That means no seams in a typical kitchen; and with no seams, there's no place for dirt to lodge.

Spangled with starbursts. Is it possible to achieve color coordination even when the colors don't precisely match? Yes. The solution is to select colors that harmonize without conflict. Here the colorful starbursts in the rotogravure floor covering are also found, in a smaller scale, on the insides of the window shades. That's where the theme begins. Elsewhere we find hues that fit the mix without actually duplicating it. The cupboards, the painted bamboo-pattern furniture, even the cooking utensils contribute to the overall effect.

Theater in the round. When your home is perched in the middle of gorgeous scenery, you should take advantage of it. In fact, you may be able to turn every room into a special viewing location. Even the kitchen? Of course. Look at what's been done here. Storage drawers are set below a curved counter that lines the windows. Tables and lighting fixtures carry out the "round" theme. And the special insets in the vinyl tile flooring help direct the eye to the stone-surfaced patio outside, then to the lake and the mountains in the distance.

Inviting the countertops into the game. In a typical home, the kitchen is the one room with significant built-ins: the cupboards and their countertops. Because of their size they, like the flooring, become major decorating elements. In this kitchen the countertop is of a flexible vinyl material that can be coved up the wall, so there's no dirt-catching seam. It's in a design that features tiny squares of vinyl set into a clear vinyl background. This design is similar to the one in the flooring. But the countertop is closer to eye-level, so its styling is on a smaller scale.

Go with the glow. Although this sample home in Illinois is contemporary in every respect, its builder provided for a touch of Old World warmth: a brick wall that stretches along one side of the kitchen. The look of brick or natural stone adds an accent note that can distinguish many a home. The flooring of embossed vinyl sheet material extends into the dining room, providing decorative unity while it helps to make the home easier to care for.

Making good use of the space in the kitchen. If there are ways to make the work areas of the home more efficient, why not take advantage of them? Good planning went into the layout of this kitchen, and you can see how many steps that saves every day. An L-shaped counter along the wall serves the area of sink and cupboards. An island counter accommodates the kitchen range, with a ceiling-mounted vent above. Now there's even room for a breakfast area.

Ring in the Riviera. If you picked up this room by helicopter and dropped it into an Italian villa on the Mediterranean, it would feel right at home. The decorative ceramic wall tile, the stoneware on the plate rail, the painted furniture—all contribute to that La Spezia look. Which just goes to show that in a contemporary American home you can achieve decorative elegance through the right choice of furnishings. Don't overlook the flooring here. It has the appearance of expensive European tile, but it's actually a cushioned vinyl sheet material.

Chapter 2
Dining rooms

Gradually during the 1960s dining rooms became more important as places for entertaining. That meant a bit more formality, and certainly more attention to their interior design. One reason was that kitchens increasingly had become the spot for family meals. We didn't think of it this way at the time, but that was a throwback to the days of mostly rural homes, when members of the family would gather around the kitchen table to partake of fresh food grown on the farm. The dining room, now as then, was reserved for guests.

Establishing a regal atmosphere.
As this room shows, it really is possible to establish an ever-elegant setting in the home. Staking a claim to the theme here is the vinyl sheet flooring, shimmering with golden tracery. A custom inset frames the table and chairs. During the early 1960s, when Armstrong featured the room in its advertising, flooring of this type for a room twelve feet wide and fifteen feet long would have cost about $195, including installation. Louvered shutters and a display of prized porcelain ware help extend the radiance of the setting.

Intimate dining in a formal setting. In an otherwise casual home, you may wish to keep some areas more formal. Especially those rooms used for entertaining guests. As exemplified here by the richly upholstered chairs, the selection of furniture is one way to carry this off. The display of beautiful items on open shelves and even the arrangement of framed pictures on the wall add to the mood. And the light from graceful candelabra creates just the right aura for an unforgettable evening.

Going with gingham. How to set off antiques and other treasured home furnishings in a modern home? This room shows one way. It uses gingham effects, in fabric and wallpaper, to establish a long-ago feeling of easy comfort. On the wall is framed an intricate Pennsylvania German *Scherenschnitte*, or paper cutting. The fringed border on the tablecloth and the decorative awning outside the window help to further the nostalgic theme.

Special touches perform decorative magic. Window walls frame the greenery of potted plants and trees outside, helping to achieve the unity of one uninterrupted space. Furthering the idea is the "weathered brick" flooring. Actually, it's linoleum in a realistic (but much more practical) simulation. The lighting fixture above the dining table generates plenty of illumination in a soft, non-obtrusive way. On the patio, the wicker chairs have "pop-up" backs. When rain threatens, you simply fold them down against the padded chair seats; the two form a handle by which you can easily carry the chairs indoors.

Cheerful is the room where the tulips are in bloom. Almost everything about this setting says, "Welcome! Come on in!" The gingham-like wallpaper and the repeat of the stencil designs near the ceiling. The cutouts in the shaped chairbacks and the fringed tablecloth, which are echoed in the children's area beside the window. The bird cage in a well-lit corner at left. And especially the custom-designed tulip insets in the floor. This vinyl sheet flooring features pebble-like chips, like natural stone fragments, in random shapes. Its surface is gently textured rather than glossy like a mirror. That's intentional, because the texture helps to hide streaks and provides a more interesting visual effect.

Provincial splendor stretches from room to room. Heirloom furnishings and colonial print fabrics collude in room groupings that are comfortable to live with and easy to care for. The mosaic-like design in the vinyl sheet flooring, with custom-cut insets, enhances the warmth of the overall setting. This floor styling also contributes a feeling of spaciousness when it's used, as it is here, to unite several rooms.

Entertaining in an unforgettable environment. From the conversation pit, you step up to unquestionable elegance in this dining room. The sweeping curves set into the vinyl sheet flooring take their cue from the roundness of the dining table, the chair bases, and the vented fireplace. This setting demonstrates how the eye can be directed in interior design by the arrangement of its elements—in this instance, by the custom flooring effects that flow your attention to the view seen through a window wall.

41

The serenity of a Japanese interior. Noted for its simplicity and its graceful, well-balanced proportion is Japanese decoration. One of its secrets is to dramatize a few well-chosen objects with placement and lighting. Notice the arrangement of the bonsai tree at left, the stone sculpture in the center, and the three-stringed samisen at right. Guests sit on pillows to dine around a sunken well. Most Japanese furniture is low; in such a setting it's a good idea to pay special attention to the floor. Chosen for this room was a sheet material that features stone-like vinyl chips set into a base of deep translucent vinyl.

Repeating a favorite motif. Suppose you have a special item, bold and distinctive, around which you'd like to build your interior scheme. How do you do that? Here's one way. In this instance, the eight-petal daisy of a dining table became the pattern for the smaller version set into the vinyl sheet flooring. The sweeping, swirling curves of the flooring add further interest to the room. Can't you imagine the admiring comments of guests as they gather for a meal in such a setting?

Welcome to an English country garden. The English are noted as superb, innovative gardeners. They love to decorate indoors around garden motifs. This room shows one way to do so with a lasting impression. Statuary sets off a fountain alcove that is flanked by luxuriant flowering plants. The unusual metal furniture is ornate, in keeping with the setting, but comfortable. Such a room gives the hostess an opportunity to use her finest crystal and porcelainware. The flooring, though its beauty helps to carry out the theme, is an especially durable type; spilled garden soil is not likely to mar its surface.

Pass through here to the dining room. Having a dining room right off the foyer is unusual but not unheard of. Actually, it's quite a practical idea. Your guests can move from the home's living room through the foyer into the dining room, feeling more welcome with every step. A citrus tree waves at them as they pass through, catching a glimpse of the bentwood furniture around the table. Screens of translucent material provide some degree of privacy while admitting diffused light.

When it's time to turn toward home. Often the deepest feelings in our lives are those that call to us from our roots. A room like this, filled with echoes of the past, helps us answer the call in an always-pleasant way. Everything orbits around the enameled iron stove, of course, but the stove isn't the only thing that lends warmth to the setting. All the furnishings blend to bring the family together for good food, good conversation. Note especially the design on the window shade and in the stenciled area near the ceiling; it's copied from an Amish quilt in a pattern called "Ohio Stars."

Opposite:
Old World workmanship. This dining room is smaller than many. But it's given distinction by the skills handed down through generations of Alpine craftsmen. The heavily carved details of the table and cushioned chairs are reflected in the shelves of the wall cupboard and other furnishings. The floor styling fits the setting, too. It's a vinyl sheet material that resembles inlaid ceramic tiles, and it provides a quiet foil for the richness of the room interior.

Left:
Descent to downstairs dining. As the family expands and the space in the home seems to become smaller as a result, it may be time to look for offbeat solutions to the problem of finding room for everything. Here's an answer that works well for one family: fit out a family room as a dining area suitable for guests. The furnishings are simple, yet homey and comfortable. And everything is chosen for easy maintenance. Spills, for example, wipe up readily from the vinyl sheet flooring in a slate-like design.

Music to follow. Formal dining flows from this theme, based on Polish decorating, in which every element adds to the atmosphere. The carved architectural brackets at the ceiling, the sconces that add a lambent glow to the sparkle of the chandelier, the graceful curves built into the vinyl flooring—all play a part in establishing a noble theme. An adjoining solarium is fitted out as a music room, to assure that guests enjoy an evening they'll remember with pleasure.

Shh! This ceiling is quietly hiding cracked plaster.
That's right. Concealed behind this attractive overhead surface is an old plaster ceiling that's cracked, peeling and discolored. Installing ceiling tiles like these is the simple way to resolve such a problem. The new acoustical ceiling soaks up a lot of the noise that strikes it, and that makes for happier, more restful mealtimes. Back in 1960, Armstrong advertised that all the material for this ceiling, eleven by fourteen feet in size, would cost about $45; and a do-it-yourselfer could install it.

The murmur of the sounding sea. What better way to welcome guests in a seaside home than to serve them dinner with a wide-open view of the surf? Scroll-cut doors lead to the setting, whose elegance is amplified by the chandelier above the table. The marble-like flooring of a vinyl sheet material, with its soft glitter and intriguing tracery of veins, helps to complete the beauty of this home interior without detracting from the exterior scene.

A maharajah's magic. The intrigue of pre-independence India imbues this room. The elegant silhouette designs in the furnishings, the carefully chosen accouterment, even the antique birdcage over the dining table (live bird not currently in residence!), all contribute to the exotic beauty of the setting. In the vinyl flooring, custom designs suggestive of Shalimar lotus blossoms are skillfully set into the surface. In the flooring itself, grained stone-like fragments are nestled within a translucent grout. The result is a nubbly texture you can actually feel.

A room that creates its own art. Just as the proper setting heightens the beauty of a jewel, so this room sets off the well-chosen treasures it contains. The wrought iron divider screens reveal what at first glance they seem to conceal. French Provincial furniture promises a meal that's as elegant as its surroundings. Glass doors at the far end of the room provide a glimpse of sculpture, profiled against the lighted cityscape in the distance. Underlying everything is the flooring, a sheet material comprising stone-like chips of vinyl set into a translucent vinyl base. Each chip is veined in natural colors. The surface looks pebbly and feels nubbly. And because the flooring comes in sheets, it can be installed in a room like this with few seams.

Any home can become a lanai. The beauty of nature plays a large part in Hawaiian decorating. See how this room combines the textures of carved wood, wickerwork, and polished stones into a unified whole that remains open and inviting. Flowering shrubs and trees, inside and out, add a new dimension. So does the vinyl sheet flooring, with its custom-cut inset that suggests a rose bursting into bloom. Though the inset is large, it doesn't overpower the setting because its coloration is subtle and its outlines are graceful. The screens, patterned like a dragon-fly's wing, add a delicate, airy atmosphere. When they're chosen with care, the furnishings in such a "theme room" can add to its intrigue.

A llama would llove it! And who wouldn't? This room offers so much of interest, all inspired by Peruvian folk art. Designs from the land of the Incas are noted for their strength and texture. Combined here with authentic art treasures are hand-embossed ceramic work, carved wooden furniture, and rich coloration inspired by that of the Peruvian highlands. Even the tableware is of that area. Though such decorating may call for a dash of daring, the result is indelible excitement. And that excitement transfers itself to the whole meal when guests come to dine in a setting like this.

Royal dining from the land of the shahs. Iranian decoration, tracing back to its Persian origins, is characterized by arches, intricate ornamentation, and elaborate furnishings. Such richness of spirit is exemplified in this setting, which focuses on a lavishly spread table that is sunk within a dining well. A caution: when your guests will be seated with the floor practically at eye level, it's important that the floor be spotless. That's why a sheet vinyl type of flooring, which can be installed with few seams in a room this size, makes good sense. When guests are expected, its surface can be swished clean with a damp mop.

Visualize a night in Vienna. Pulling up memories from the past helps to create a graceful atmosphere for dining. Here the romance of nineteenth century Vienna is suggested by gilded mirrors, satin, and filigree work, blended into an evocative whole. The centerpiece of the room is the dining table, surrounded by matching wooden chairs. Setting off this focal point are a latticework "cage" and a flowered geometric area rug. In the adjoining kitchen, an elaborately decorated range hood helps to carry out the theme, as do flounces at the tops of the windows.

Open to suggestion. Visualize the possibilities in an informal dining area like this one. Situated just off the kitchen, it offers convenience as well as conversation-inspiring decorative ideas that originated in the kraals of sub-Saharan Africa. After they dine, guests or members of the family can take their ease on the brightly-hued couch that lines the wall beneath the window. For a cooler-weather get-together, there's a vented fireplace at right. Rich, bold patterns and a variety of surface textures are typical of African design, and you'll find them here.

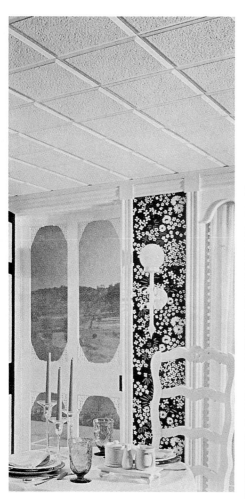

Far left:
Room with a view—straight up. An unsightly ceiling detracts from any room's appearance. It isn't difficult to correct that problem in a way that adds a new and sometimes forgotten surface to the decorative treatment. This ceiling tile, which is suitable for installation by a do-it-yourselfer, has deeply beveled edges that make it look expensive. But it's not. When Armstrong featured the ceiling tile in an advertisement of the late 1960s, the company said that ceiling material of this type for a room 12 feet wide and 14 feet long would cost about $42.

Left:
The pretty way to peace and quiet. See those random swirls in the ceiling? They're embossed into its surface, and the secret they bear is that they soak up a lot of the noise that's generated during mealtime. That makes for easier, more restful conversation. This type of ceiling tile is designed for installation by the do-it-yourselfer. What's more, it can be painted, so the ceiling is as easy to keep up as it is to put up. Here the tiles are installed in an ashlar fashion, and the design is a pleasing complement to the rather elaborate chandelier and to the open, shelved cabinet along the far wall.

The dining room that never goes to waste. This room has so much to offer. Guests can relax and enjoy themselves here in surroundings as comfortable as they look. But when the room is not being used for meals or entertaining, it doubles as a family room. There's space for the lively, noisy activities, such as music-making or television-watching, in which all members of the family join. Quieter pursuits are also provided for, with a quiet corner where one may answer correspondence. The room even offers a display case for cherished antique glass collectibles.

Right on the money. It's a Colonial look with a stop-'em-in-their tracks twist. If you want to do something daringly different in your dining room decoration, consider this change of pace. It got its start from the appearance of an Early American tavern, then took off from there. The coins are cast aluminum replicas of the 1878 silver dollar. They're set into a sheet vinyl material in two contrasting colors, custom-installed with an inviting swirl that leads diners to the table.

Can a floor this rich-looking come out of a box? Absolutely. It's a vinyl-content tile that was developed with the do-it-yourselfer in mind. He spreads the adhesive with a brush, then presses each block into place (see inset). The tile has a handsome medallion embossed into its surface. But, because it's laid one block at a time, the home handyman can readily create his own special flooring effects. Here he has combined the main pattern with plainer tiles of complementary colors to help separate the room areas while still maintaining decorative unity.

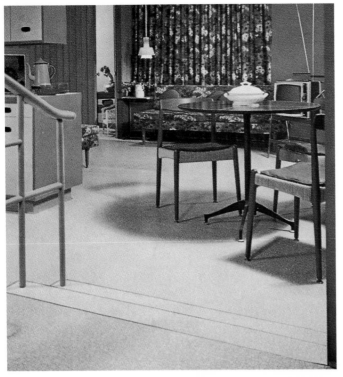

The dining room that's not ashamed to call a kitchen its neighbor. Far from it. In fact, the dining chairs borrow the blue of their padding from the accent patches found in the kitchen. In these informal rooms, color is used to especially telling effect. The drapery fabric on the far wall is also applied to the upholstery fabric of the chair peeking out at left. The flooring throughout, in a subtle coloration of vinyl sheet material, provides a quiet undercurrent that lets the more vivid hues speak their piece without conflict. A couple of railed steps assure a dramatic entry into this area of the home.

Open up and let the sunshine in. Imagine sitting down to a meal in a room that never loses its cheer. No wonder guests like to linger here! Daylight comes pouring through the window-wall, burnishing the leaves of potted plants and bathing the whole interior with a glowing radiance. In planning such a space, it's important to consider maintenance, for you want the room to retain its happy smile. A floor of sheet vinyl material helps to assure that the room will be easy to keep clean. Spills wipe up readily from its surface, which is embossed for an added decorative appeal.

Wicker wonderland. The imaginative selection of furnishings can transform almost any room in the home into a more attractive space. Note how the wicker-and-bamboo effects of the breakfast room furniture are carried through the entire setting. Now the room is comfortable, fashionable, appealing in every way. Establishing a decorative base for the furnishings is the floor. It's a vinyl sheet material with an embossed surface, suggesting a patio of random, textured stones on the sun-drenched shores of the Mediterranean. Lavishly spread through the room, flowering plants complete the scene.

See-through furniture. Don't demur at daring differences. Let's say that you come across a style of furniture that seems outré. Yet you feel that you could make it work in that certain room of yours. Go right ahead. Chances are good that, if you feel comfortable with the choice, it'll fit fine in your home. Such is the case in this dining area. It's wide open, with the sunlight rushing in through those capacious windows. And see how well the transparent table and chairs match up. They help to convey the atmosphere of elegant invitation that pervades the space. Even the counter, with its pass-through to the kitchen, doesn't interrupt the flow of sight through the space. The flooring, a Spanish tile design in vinyl sheet form, adds its own sparkle to the whole effect.

Chapter 3
Living rooms

At one time the living room was the spot for family members to cluster after dinner. Now, with family rooms having gained rapid acceptance beginning in the mid-1950s, they were taking on this role in the American home. This meant that living rooms could be reduced in size, and one often finds this to be the case in houses built in the '60s. In this chapter look for the ways in which Armstrong subtly showed how to make a small living room look larger—particularly through the treatment of the resilient flooring.

A sophisticated sonata of high style. A room can make a first impression, just as a person can. When it's a room in your own home, you want that initial glance to be favorable. How could anyone not be struck by the elegance and good taste of this living room? The placement of the furniture, the well-chosen painting beside the grand piano, the sense of style the setting conveys, all reflect the highest aesthetic values. But practicality hasn't been ignored. The space includes an easy-to-maintain vinyl sheet floor and a noise-quieting acoustical ceiling.

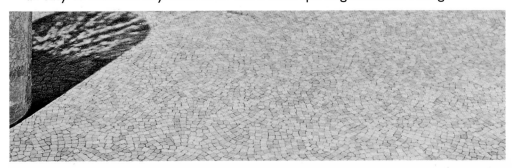

Mighty nice to come home to. After dining with friends at a fashionable restaurant, now you're home again. You leave your purse and your gloves on the table just inside the entryway, you drape your scarf on a chair, and you look around. As always, you're struck by the attractiveness of your home interior. You are pleased that you selected the furnishings not just for their beauty but also for the quiet comfort they provide you. And you know that you will never tire of them.

Light, bright, and informal. One view of modern interior design has it that such design is successful if you can visualize yourself living with it comfortably, year in and year out. If that's the criterion, then certainly this room would qualify as good interior design. It's informal, yet tasteful in every way. Its straight vertical lines are offset by the cozy-looking curves of the tables and chairs. The draperies admit a fine view of the patio just outside but may be drawn to provide privacy when that's called for.

Come on down for convivial conversation. Here's a home that clearly was made for friendly visits. The curve of the brass balustrade leads you right to the fireplace, and the room is laid out concentrically from this focal point. A row of arches frames the luxuriant plant growth just outside the window walls. The lighting is soft and indirect but more than adequate for reading and other quiet pursuits. The flooring is of vinyl, with brass insets that outline the sweep of the conversation pit.

Unleash your imagination. With a bit of foresight, artifacts gathered from many parts of the world can be combined in an interesting manner. That's illustrated by the eclectic furnishings in this setting. All come together in a pleasant, unified blend. The flooring helps. It's a sheet vinyl featuring random-sized chips that resemble pebbles. The surface is pebbly, too. You can feel the texture. That and its finish, which is lustrous without being mirror-shiny, help conceal scuff marks and dents from pointed heels.

It takes a touch of brass. This lakeside villa was positioned to take advantage of the natural outdoor beauty with which it is blessed. Wide-awake window-walls open the home's eyes to a memorable vista. The narrow planking on the underside of the verandah seems to direct one's attention to the view. Inside, the glow of brass in the candelabra and in the three-footed table at right contrast pleasantly with the wooden "spiderleg" table at center stage.

Rustic or sleek? Which is it? Breathtaking at first glance, this dramatic interior merits a second look because it offers so much of interest. With its heavy wooden uprights taken from a barn that was being dismantled, its antique door hardware, and its natural stone fireplace, the room suggests country decorating at its best. But wait a minute. The polished marble, the vinyl flooring with arching insets, especially the construction of the conversation pit—these all point toward a dedication to modern comfort and convenience. It's a room that defies easy categorization. But doesn't it all work beautifully?

Wild as the driven wind. Looking out onto a scene of openness and grandeur, this interior calls on the tortured branches of a bonsai tree, the cut-out panels of the divider screens to capture the wildness of nature. Yet there's a serenity in the room itself. Part of the answer lies in its spaciousness. You'll never feel crowded here, never feel constrained by your surroundings. The geometric insets of the vinyl flooring help direct your eye to a grouping of furniture that's arranged for quiet conversation.

Making a small apartment more livable. Space is limited here. But the interior is so well laid out that you'd hardly notice that. At left is the living room, with comfortable furniture and rich, dark paneling to make it more inviting. Dividers hide the well-lighted bedroom area at right. Note how the two spaces are tied together decoratively by several design elements: the openwork metal screens on the dividers and at the top of the door, the style of furniture, and the stretch of vinyl flooring in a coloration that attractively sets off the apartment's other furnishings.

For people who are hung up on wood. If you like the warmth that a touch of wood gives to a living room, here's a ceiling that you'll find appealing. The usual way to put up a suspended ceiling is to hang a white metal grid by wires from your old ceiling, then lay the ceiling panels right on top of the grid. But the type of grid-riser shown here, made of walnut-grained steel, raises the panels three-quarters of an inch above the grid. The result is a ceiling that has striking dimension, accented by the richness of wood.

Diagonals add excitement to a traditional interior. This room relies on strongly slanted geometric effects to lend an air of spice to an otherwise quiet setting, with essentially a horizontal look. The lines of the painting are reflected in the area rug, which is reminiscent of a "penny" rug homemade by the Amish. Underlying everything is a resilient tile floor in taupe tones that complement the other furnishings.

As comfortable to visit as to live in. The coffee service is already in place on the round table at center, so we know that company's expected. But look around, and you'll readily see why this room makes family members as welcome as visitors. Well-appointed as it is, there's nothing "off limits" about it. A cheery fire behind the pull-open brass fan firescreen, furniture chosen for its practicality as well as its beauty, and pleasant views of the outdoors make this a living room that truly is designed for living.

Would you believe that this is a mobile home? Well, it is! And it demonstrates that, with planning and a good decorative sense applied to it, even the limited space of manufactured housing can present an interior that's entirely livable as well as pleasing to the eye. Note the attention given to window treatment, lighting, and the selection of carpet and other furnishings.

Do not disturb. It's just right as it is. The furniture is well-selected, from the low Parsons table at center to the contemporary pieces around the edges of the room. The carpet is rich and tasteful without being over-costly. The lighting is placed to encourage a variety of activities, including quiet conversation with guests. Did we say "quiet"? Our friend relaxing at left will appreciate that!

More than just the top of a room. Sometimes it seems that the only time you notice a ceiling is when there's something wrong with it. In an otherwise elegant interior, a ceiling that's stained, cracked, or peeling can ruin the whole effect. But a modern type of ceiling tile, designed for installation by the do-it-yourselfer, hides the flaws. Some types can be suspended below the old ceiling, and these can even conceal pipes and other structural features. The result is that now the ceiling, too, becomes a decorative element in the room.

Elegantly embroidered. A room that speaks softly of good taste can be formal without being stuffy. It's a space in which you can follow such quiet pursuits as reading, writing, and needle-work without ever feeling cramped. Here the floor is a vinyl material in sheet form. That means almost no seams in a living room this size, and that in turn means no places for dirt to hide. On the far wall, bookshelves are backed with wallpaper in a floral design, offsetting the granite-chip texture of the flooring and the monochromatic walls and built-in cupboards.

Modern convenience in an Early American room? Colonial furnishings have enduring good looks. But to some people, decorating in an Early American style can be intimidating. Can you maintain the effect you want without sacrificing desirable modern touches? Let's face it. Almost any decorator accepts certain compromises. Electric lamps, for example. In this living room, the flooring is a modern type of vinyl-content tile that offers easy mainte-nance. And it's a fine complement to the braided rug and the furniture pieces that dress the room.

Cordiality when company comes to call. The living room of this poolside home waves a welcome to any guest who comes through the door. Its warmth starts with the parquet beauty of its flooring, a natural cork tile with a wear layer of clear vinyl. The tile is accented with brass insets. The flooring helps to unify the overall decorating scheme as it stretches into the dining room at left and (see below) down the hallway to other parts of the home. Furnishings are spare but comfortable, and a grouping of framed pictures on one wall adds interest.

Chapter 4

Bedrooms

During the 1960s Armstrong furthered its bedroom design innovations, which had proven so popular in the preceding decade. Here you'll find theme rooms, rooms designed just for girls or just for boys, and rooms that sparkle with a special touch of gentility. One of the bedrooms features a color-laden "hat bar" dressing table; another, a set of seafarer's hammocks at the foot of the beds; still another, Eskimo art to lend an unforgettable touch. Watch especially for the space-saving ideas this chapter includes.

A built-in canopy bed. If you want to do something different and rather grand in a bedroom, here's an idea to consider. See how partitioning gives this part of the room its own special character. The curtains may be drawn closed along a recessed track to make this area as private as any canopied bed could do. Decorative unity is provided by the scrollwork that runs along the top of the bed, then bends at a right angle to frame the large windows, as well as by an attractive flooring in a design that features mosaic-like vinyl squares.

Safari, so good. For the two young boys who live in this home, every night is a trek into the bush. Waking to such a setting starts each morning with excitement. Springy, comfortable wicker chairs, coupled with authentic African masks and other handicrafts, make this a room they'll never tire of. Note the effective use of bamboo and the fringed adornment of the lower bunk. A faux leopard-skin rug is laid over the vinyl sheet flooring, which has insets suggestive of Swahili spears. Hey! Don't go out in the sun without your pith helmet!

Topping off the bedroom with a new idea. Even a simple step, well carried off, can add zest to the ordinary bedroom. Try this on for size: a "hat bar" dressing table at one end of the room. Well, sure, it's a practical idea for the woman who loves her hats and enjoys choosing just the right one for today's outing. But it's also a way to add color and form to a room that in a decorating sense sometimes threatens to go flat.

Out of the park. The sun's always shining in this bedroom for an especially active boy, thanks to the bright area rug. It's laid over a floor that looks like random-width wooden planks but actually is embossed linoleum in a realistic-looking effect. A couch that turns into a bed clings close to the wall, and that gives the occupant plenty of room to swing a baseball bat when Mom's not looking. There's also room for trophies on the little table at right and room for homework at the desk against the far wall. At left, racks keep autograph-model bats at the ready.

Sugar and spice—and everything's nice. She's just a little girl, but oh so feminine. She fits just right into this bedroom, with its ribbons and bows and swags of fabric. It provides her a dressing table of her own, makes her feel like a true princess in her canopy bed, and gives her plenty of room when her friends come for a visit. An antique baby carriage becomes a home for a favorite doll. The vinyl sheet flooring, with its pink and golden spangles glittering in their softly colored background, is of a type that can be installed in any level of the home: upstairs, at ground level, or downstairs.

Home for the sailor, home from the sea. Designed for two boys who love the adventures of the open sea, this room has plenty to keep them occupied. Its furnishings include, at left, a navigation table and, at right, a refinished masthead double block that serves as a low table. The "hammocks" at the end of each bed are handy for storage of hobby items and small items of clothing, to help keep the place shipshape. The compass rose set into the flooring doubles as a game board. The boys themselves tied the various sailor's knots framed on the far wall.

Basketfuls of bliss. What little girl wouldn't find pleasure in a bedroom that's clearly designed with her in mind? It's polka dots and wicker all the way. But of course all those baskets are more than decorative. They provide easy-access storage bins for dolls, toys, and games to keep them out of the way when they're not being used. Even water-color spills don't damage the vinyl sheet flooring; they wipe up with a whisk of a damp cloth. This flooring has a gently textured surface that helps hide scuffs and other marks.

Unapologetically rustic. Here's a room that proudly proclaims its resident camper's interest in outdoor pursuits. The honors he won as a Cub Scout are on display, and so are the results of his knot-tying efforts. There's even a sure-enough tree, so he has a branch from which to hang his canteen. At left, the rope ladder leading to the upper bunk is one he made himself. A flap of canvas makes going to bed like camping out. The room has its practical side, too. It has an acoustical ceiling to keep a lid on noise, and the vinyl flooring sweeps clean easily.

Concentrate on a corner. It isn't always necessary to think in broad, sweeping terms to do something special in a home. Even simple ideas can be developed into festive themes. In this nursery, for example, attention was lavished on just one corner, and with what results! The newly created playpen has its own windows looking out onto an indoor "garden," and a quarter-round pad provides comfort and warmth. The ribbons and bows, which add a dainty touch, are echoed in the brass ribbon insets installed in the vinyl sheet flooring. The framed photograph is kept low, at a child's-eye height.

Helping two girls to make the most of it. When limited space is a problem, as in this France-inspired bedroom for two girls, the solution can be found in artful imagining. Here closets flank the sleeping area and enable each occupant to maintain her own space. Each has a bureau, too, with shelves and drawers. Flowered wallpaper even on the ceiling ties together the decor, as does the vinyl sheet flooring. Perhaps most important, an old-fashioned idea brought up to date is found in the space-saving truckle beds. Duck your head, little lamb, we're putting you in for the day!

Land of the midnight fun. Home for a pair of active boys, this upstairs bedroom has to weather a lot of growing up. Fortunately the Eskimo art, collected from around the Bering Sea, is almost as durable as it is attractive. It adds colorful accents to an area that also provides space for play.

For such a room, it's important to choose materials that not only look beautiful but also stay beautiful. Here vinyl sheet flooring, in contrasting colors for an unusual custom installation, fills the bill. The inlaid vinyl chips create a rich texture that helps hide scuff and heel marks.

Bright white overhead for a cheerful setting. In this bedroom for a girl, special thought has been given to making everything dashing and inviting. The walls and molding are painted to coordinate with the bows on the curtains and with the pillows on the bed. The ceiling, though, is white—a brilliant white, to serve as a foil for the colorful furnishings. This ceiling, with its richly textured surface, is one that do-it-yourselfers can install. Alongside the window, shelves are provided for an array of potted flowers.

A room for boys that can grow as they do. On the second floor of this home, a spacious area has been set aside for the young men of the family. Right now they're adolescents, but it's designed to remain useful as they add years and change their interests. Each boy has his own study desk—one by the window, the other tucked behind the bookshelves at right. A shelf extending from the upper bunk provides space for special possessions and for just-before-sleep reading material. There's room for play in this room, too, and under everything is a vinyl floor that will stand up to rough treatment.

Chapter 5
Bathrooms

A typical home built in the 1960s, unlike those of the '50s, had at least one powder room in addition to the main bathroom. Another idea gaining prominence was that of the bathroom with a stall shower instead of a bathtub. In designing its interiors, Armstrong concentrated on the master bathroom. It showed how you can start with the layout of the fixtures, then turn your imagination loose to create a room that your family will enjoy using and that visitors to your home will find inspiringly beautiful. Yes, the bathroom!

Open to the sky. Watch for hovering helicopters when it's shower time in this bathroom! Sunlight comes flooding in through the slanted windows to make this always a pleasant place to spend your time. Towel racks, strategically near the bathtub, are designed to facilitate air-drying. A screen with a stylized leaf-covered tree adds a touch of the outdoors, as do the potted fern and the fresh-cut flowers at left. The flooring features gently colored vinyl chips set at random into clear vinyl. Note how it's coved up alongside the tub enclosure, so there's no sharp corner to catch dirt. On the far wall, a framed floral print adds a colorful touch.

Left and below:

Elegant good taste in a small space. Even when space is limited, it's possible to achieve fashionable design. In a bathroom, it's almost essential to start with the choice and placement of the fixtures, then plan around those. Here the sleek smoothness of the tub and lavatory is offset by the natural wood-grain found in the cabinet. The brass drawer pulls are complemented by the four-point-star insets in the vinyl sheet flooring. On the counter, a tray of bath oils also contains a basket of straw flowers for a fragrant rustic touch. Behind the screen at lower right is the room's heating element. Towels are stored in this cupboard area, so when the weather turns chilly they're warm anytime you want to use them.

The splendor of a Mediterranean villa. A forerunner of the saunas that would become popular in future years, a sunken bath is the focal point of this 1960s interior. The arched niches frame a mural of the sea and repeat the curve of the doorway that leads to the outdoors. The flooring, a sheet material with tiny squares of vinyl set into a clear vinyl grout, suggests the hand-laid tesserae found in Europe. Storage cabinets flank the well-lighted dressing table at right, and a comfortable chair is at hand for someone who may wish to spend leisure time here.

Just off the master bedroom. This bedroom, with its ruffled canopy bed, has a private bath close by. And private it is. Louvered doors with spring hinges keep the bathroom fixtures hidden away. Flocculated wallpaper adds a touch of luxury to the setting, and the floor is worth a special mention. It's a vinyl sheet type that offers a light, almost pure white background and color accents that complement the other furnishings to complete the decorative scheme. These have been coordinated with the popular colors in bath fixtures, towels, kitchen appliances, countertop materials, ceramic tile, and drapery fabrics. This simplifies color selection in decorating.

The opulence of Carrara marble. Well, at least the handsome *appearance* of Carrara marble. But the flooring in this bath, which carries into the adjoining room to set the decorating tone for the entire suite, is in several ways a more practical choice for the home than marble would be. It isn't as cold and hard underfoot, it's easy to clean, and it comes in a selection of subtle colors. A step-down tub, a foldaway brass towel rack, and a dressing table with lots of storage space give this room the comfortable, rich feel of an Italian *palazzo*. If you like to pamper yourself occasionally, what better setting in which to do that!

Chapter 6
Family rooms, recreation rooms, and dens

The 1960s was the first decade during which most homes being built could boast of family rooms. The transition had occurred since World War II. Dens had evolved into television-watching rooms (sometimes with a recreation-room flavor). Now came the family room: larger, with more attention paid not just to television but also to the special interests of all members of the family. Armstrong was quick to recognize the importance of the change, and it presented an abundance of ideas for well-designed family rooms.

Stand fast! The children are coming! In this multilevel home, young children are given freedom to do almost anything they want to do in the family room. Even with rough play, there's little they could think of that would cause serious damage here. The flooring is a vinyl sheet material that readily sweeps clean. And good use is made of a durable patio table, replete with striped umbrella, here set at a height for entertaining playmates. By the window are storage spaces for toys, so the room can be made neat as an infantry barracks when playtime is ended.

Oriental simplicity. American practicality. Universal beauty. The unusual fireplace, with its space for cooking, takes center stage here. See how the other furnishings seem to cluster around it. An authentic Japanese lantern illuminates the collection of Asian dolls on the shelf in the background, and dark rough-hewn timbers provide an attractive frame for the setting. If you're going to invite your guests to seat themselves on floor cushions, you'd better have a special flooring. And this one *is* special. It's a sheet material featuring thousands of tiny vinyl squares set into a clear vinyl grout.

Quiet—it's an active room for the whole family. Almost by definition, a family room is one that should be open to everyone in the household, and with few restrictions on the activities that take place there. But for this very reason, noise can build up to an uncomfortable level. Not likely in this room. Its acoustical ceiling soaks up much of the noise that strikes it. And the one-by-four-foot lengths of a ceiling material that resembles wood paneling become a part of the decoration. An unusual hanging light fixture adds to the effect.

A trip to the South Seas, any day or night. Here's a room fitted out for entertaining guests. But members of the family enjoy spending their time here, too. It's a simple matter to prepare food at the vented grille on the lanai, then to whisk it inside through the sliding door. How at ease you feel when sitting on the cushions to dine! The kitchen is nearby for convenience in preparing and serving more elaborate meals. Stylized frangipani blossoms, set into the vinyl sheet flooring, help to carry out the theme, as does the fabric of the cushions.

Hot hors d'oeuvres on tap. You step down into this unusual family room; and when you do, you find it's all ready for you. The vented hood over the low table facilitates food preparation right on the spot. Custom flooring insets radiating from the table carry out the design of its wrought-iron scrollwork. Guests relax on the comfortable seating while enjoying the ever-changing view of the water beyond the deck. At the corners of the couch, the finials take the form of pineapples, the universal symbol of hospitality.

Go native, but go in style. Come you back to Mandalay in this interior inspired by tea plantations along the banks of the Irrawaddy. Inspect the comfort couched in this room and you'll recognize that you're never far from civilization here. Of special interest are the cowled "emperor chairs" made of wicker, each with its own overhead lamp and its swing-away tray for holding dinnerware. On the deck outside, windscreens anchored at their corners frustrate heavy breezes while admitting a certain degree of light through their translucent fabric.

Where the teen-agers hang out, right at home. In the pre-compact disc days of the 1960s, plenty popular were 45-rpm records. Here's a theme room that builds on that popularity. Records, easily removable for dropping onto the turntable, climb their way up a divider screen. Even the custom inset in the vinyl flooring goes for the record! Swivel chairs at the built-in soda fountain make this a place for after-school entertaining, a place any teen-ager would be proud to invite his or her friends to share. Park your bike outside and come on in.

A rolling river of rhythm. All the disparate elements of this room harmonize in a way that says, "Here's a place for lighthearted enjoyment." Dominating everything is the old-fashioned carousel horse. The stripes on its supporting pole are reflected in those of the draperies and in the swirling effect in gold, brown, and green custom-set into the vinyl floor. At right, the stools pick up the design of the chess set in an appropriate way. And the chair in the background is provided with plenty of light for reading.

Bower for bird-watchers. This step-down family room is close to the leafy slice of nature right outside the window. It's well-designed for observing feathered denizens of the area (as the friendly porcelain cat in the background would agree!). It's a place for quiet study and contemplation. But it's also fine for entertaining guests. Storage cupboards are provided under the window, and a South American wind chime adds a spontaneous musical flavor to the whole interior when the breeze comes in.

Winter finds its way to warmth. What could be more fitting than knitting? Especially in a setting like this. With a bulbous pot-bellied stove taking center stage on its brick pedestal, the room is cozy even on the coldest of days. Sunlight splashes into the corners through its well-positioned windows, and a supply of firewood is at hand for ready replenishment. At right a tea table is set up for informal entertaining of guests. The furnishings are practical, too. For example, consider the vinyl sheet flooring. Everything from ashes to snippets of yarn sweep up easily from its surface.

Brightening the built-ins. Book shelves and other decorating elements that are fixed permanently in place offer definite advantages. But sometimes they can make a room seem heavy and static. Here's a solution to that problem: open up the space through the lavish use of windows. See how the sunlight floods through the entire area. Now it's bright and inviting. The dark window trim echoes the natural woods of the bookcase and the paneling. The flooring is of dark, medium, and light colorings of a design that features varicolored vinyl "pebbles" set into a translucent vinyl.

Staking a claim for simple dignity. How free, how open is this interior! There's a place for everything, yet it provides plenty of room for warmth and quiet comfort. The fireplace along the far wall forms the natural gathering place for friends and family members alike. Then, when it's time for dinner, they can make the easy transition to the dining room adjoining. Window draperies, furniture, even the large framed painting were chosen with care to enhance the overall effect of quality and good taste.

Highlighting a piece of art. The owners of this home picked out a special place for a favorite sculpture, then made the most of it. The floor is one of the largest decorating elements in a room, and when it's used imaginatively it can become one of the most important. Here four colors in a vinyl sheet flooring create concentric rings that place the airy figure of the dancing girl right at center stage. It's impossible to overlook the sculpture when you enter the room. Other furnishings, including the stone of the fireplace and the rough texture of the natural wood, help carry out the theme.

Opposite:

In a room ready for relaxation, rack 'em up. Not every home, admittedly, has a main-floor family room large enough to accommodate billiards. But it's a leisure-time activity that's important to the family members who reside here, and they made sure to fit it in. Furthermore, they made the billiard table and its accessories a part of the decorating scheme. The cue rack, for example, becomes a room divider. When the game is over for the evening, what better place to relax than in the low-slung chairs grouped around the hearth?

Left:

A dedication to informality. A home that overlooks a golf course speaks to us of luxuriousness. Yet this one nicely reflects the family's desire to retain an inviting, informal atmosphere. One quality that helps is this room's openness, with the spaciousness of the outdoors just beyond the windows. There's something else, too. Look at the flooring. Chips of vinyl, colorfully grained like fragments of natural stone, are set into deep, translucent vinyl to form intriguing random patterns. This floor is easy to sweep clean. Let the divots fall where they may!

A trip to the Adirondacks. It's rusticity made practical and comfortable. Natural textures, such as stone, wicker, and wood—even the bark of a tree in its raw state—dominate the setting. But this interior is done with such style and grace that you immediately feel at ease with it. Living with such a room calls for furnishings that don't call for a lot of upkeep, and that's been considered here. The flooring, for example, is a type of vinyl sheet material that's easy to whisk clean with a broom or a damp mop. Above the windows at right, a shelf holds earthenware that well complements the furnishings.

Making the most of a small space. What do you do when your family room is, let's face it, *squeezed* for space? Well, you begin by eliminating the word "small" from your thinking. Instead, substitute the word "cozy" and go to work. Make use of built-ins, such as the television set in this room. Use folding screens, which can take up less space than full doors. Choose the furnishings with care, and group them compactly. Here, the flooring helps, too. It's a vinyl tile that's as lustrous as deep-quarried marble.

Suited for a man's taste. Spending an evening in this family room is, for the man of the house, like enjoying the comfort of a British club without ever leaving home. Capturing the warm feeling of a provincial interior is not difficult when you select the right furnishings. Here embossed linoleum in an Old World tile effect provides the right background for the masculine oak furniture. It also complements the brick fireplace and the floor-to-ceiling windows of the home. The woman of the house likes this room, too. That chair next to the hearth is reserved for her.

Indoors or out? Choose your spot.
Guests being entertained on a summery evening can flow from this family room to the deck just outside the sliding glass doors. The home is designed not to be confining, and that facilitates hospitality wherever people elect to congregate. A modern sculpture depending from the ceiling is similar to a larger wall-hung piece, and that helps provide decorative unity to the whole ensemble. So does the sweep of the vinyl flooring, with its variegated pebble-like chips set into a translucent vinyl grout.

Eye-level ingleside. When you're relaxing in your rocker on a crisp winter's evening, what more welcome sight than a glowing fire on the hearth? Especially if that hearth is at the level of your eyes, where it can be enjoyed the more as it spreads its warmth and light across the room! This fireplace has room beneath it for firewood, and its chimney is hidden by the partition it's mounted into. The up-and-off-the-floor location keeps it out of the way of small children playing nearby.

The Canadian side of the family is heard from. This room derives its inspiration from a hunting lodge in Canada. Of course a weekend retreat in the north woods is not really supposed to represent comfort, right? This one does! Relax on that bearskin banquette and you're looking right into the fireplace. Pierced-metal lamps above provide light for reading or for music practice. Nature's own materials and textures are everywhere in this setting, and an abstract custom design in the vinyl sheet flooring (see inset) accentuates the decorating theme.

Splendor in the Turkish manner. For some people, relaxation and retirement from the cares of the world are best achieved in an atmosphere completely different from whatever they're accustomed to. Here's a room such people can relate to. Reflected in its gleaming brass is ornateness that would have pleased a pasha. The molding along the side walls tracks the curvature of the intriguing shelved niches. Adding a bejeweled luminescence to the scene is a floor of vinyl tile. Its swirling paisley pattern rivals the richness of rare Eastern prayer rugs.

Left:

A framework for furnishings from afar. When treasured art pieces and design ideas are collected from distant lands, you want to set them off handsomely. The sloping walls of this family room keep your attention focused on the unusual objects it contains. Windows at the end of the room admit lots of sunlight, overcoming the darkness of the paneling. At night, multiple light fixtures that hang from above take over the illumination. The vented hearth at right adds warmth to the overall effect. The furniture is low-slung and informal, which suits this setting just fine.

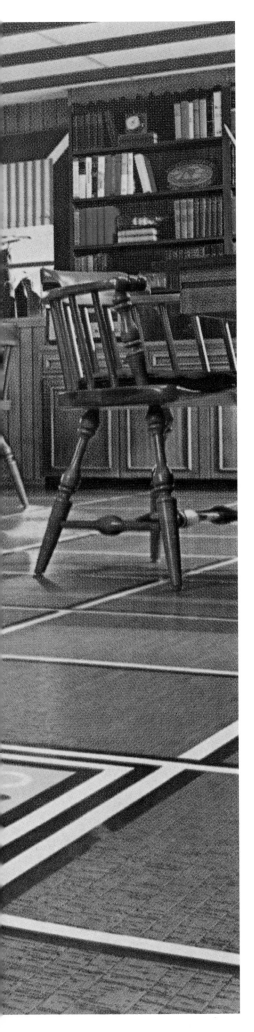

Expand ho! Broadening the home's horizons. For the family that's growing when the house is not, life can seem crowded. But sometimes it's possible to find usable space in an attic, basement, or garage. In this older home, a breezeway off the kitchen was transformed into a new family room. And not just *any* family room, but one with a theme that reflects the family's interests in nautical items. A ship's steering wheel, for example, becomes a holder for hot-pads displaying signal flags. The anchor inset in the tile floor was factory-made, ready to be installed by a do-it-yourselfer.

Like visiting a Mexican villa. Combine adobe brick, native pottery, and heavy turned Spanish furniture to capture the color of Mexico in a casual modern interior. A pass-through from the kitchen makes this a room in which your guests can enjoy an informal meal. Plenty of light is provided in the reading area at left. But here, in the main part of the space, candlelight subtly insinuates itself into the evening's plans. The vinyl sheet flooring combines two colorations in a custom design that breaks up the room into several areas.

Come on down to find your friends. This family room was once unused basement space. Now it has the ambience of a British pub. The heavy hobnailed furniture gives it a feeling of stability and security. Feature strips set into the tile flooring help to lighten the room with color and assure that it'll be simple to maintain. Want to watch television? Care for a game of draughts? Prefer a quiet evening of conversation, with just a cheerful companion or two? Your choice. In its rack at the end of the game table, your clay churchwarden pipe awaits.

I'm not here right now. I'm away on the Spanish Main. If you're planning a recreation room, go ahead and do it right. Here's one fitted out especially to meet a youngster's interest in pirates and treasure troves. He can climb a rope ladder to his own crow's nest, then use his telescope to scout the neighborhood (while a stuffed parrot looks on!). The stools are made from a ship's capstans. And the custom flooring inset becomes an intriguing treasure map in itself. If he tires of the high seas, the resident will find his baseball gear stowed neatly at right.

The conviviality of an Irish hunt club. Can you imagine a room as beautifully styled as this, in your own home? No reason not to aspire to that. What it takes is imagination, a bit of decorative daring, and a theme to start with. See how the repeated use of a few elements can establish the comfort and cheer of Ireland. The tweedy cushions, the open beams of the ceiling, the "pebbles" set into the vinyl sheet flooring. Naturally there's room for the traditional harp and the rack of long-stem pipes. And everywhere, everywhere you find trophies of the chase.

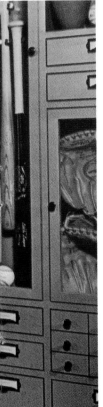

Turn it over to the teens. Problem: teen-agers' interests can differ from those of their parents (*there's* a surprise!). Solution: give the teen-agers a place of their own. That works out well in this home. Its basement has been transformed into a special place, one that's filled with opportunities for lively activities. In addition to the small raised stage for music-making, the room features its own soda fountain and several dispensing stations for snacks. The vinyl tile flooring, in a brick effect, assures that spills will be easy to swish up with a damp mop.

Don't bother me when I'm having fun. If you want to, turn yourself loose and create a room that's strictly for enjoyment. That's what this basement family room is all about. Somebody came up with that elephant's-foot table, and it all started there. Nothing's too offbeat to be accept- able here. But guess what! It works together for a practical, comfortable whole. The bentwood furniture, the more- lavish-than-usual storage space, the louvered screens, and the tile flooring all contribute to a setting that both guests and family members like to spend time in.

Opposite:
Plucked from the plains of the Southwest. Native American designs in the rug and the throw cushions set the tone for this appealing room. The sloped open-beam ceiling, the authentic old wood-stove at left, and the view to a spacious landscape suggest the life of a ranchero. It's a pleasant enough life in this setting, with its well-lighted, well-equipped kitchen adjoining. The flooring is a vinyl sheet material in a styling that suggests inlaid slabs of slate. It's easier to care for than natural slate, though, and spills wipe up without a trace.

Home for the hobby days. If a member of the family is serious about a special subject, then doesn't it make sense to devote at least a portion of the family room to that interest? Here the interest is geology, and look how beautifully the room is accommodated to that. A massive piece of quartz supports the table and becomes the focal point of the decorative theme. Shelves, drawers, and cupboards provide storage for organizing smaller mineral samples, and a sink permits cleansing of the day's field-trip find before it's added to the permanent collection.

Old World wish fulfillment. Ever dream of fixing up your basement family room so it's as inviting as a European inn? The people who live in this home did just that, making use of articles they had picked up during vacation trips. In addition to the Toby figure from the United Kingdom and the steins from Germany, there's rack-room for the pewter collection. And they've found space for an American touch, also, as the carved "barbecue" sign testifies. The tree on the bar, its branches hung with pretzels, is an idea they proudly came up with themselves.

Hear the buzz of castanets. Step down into this family room and you've taken a walk into a Spanish villa. The filigree design of the ironwork wall decoration and the Spanish tile look of the vinyl flooring provide a harmonious combination that contributes to its authentic-looking atmosphere. Often it's possible to enhance a room with a touch that appears completely natural but adds something important. The apples do that here, setting off the furnishings with their glowing color.

Opposite:
Turn it loose and let it run. In a room with an especially strong decorative element—in color, architectural detail, or furniture—it's usually best to allow that feature to dominate. The rest of the space doesn't have to compete for attention. Here the heavy turned chairs and the unusual scrollwork table call for attention and deserve it. Other elements are kept quieter. The vinyl flooring in a Mediterranean tile design performs its decorative function in a scale appropriate to the room. On the patio outside, potted geraniums lead your way up the steps.

Hideaway for grownups. In this house, here's the room in which the adults spend their evenings. Why shouldn't they? It offers just about anything they would want for their off-hours at home. Decorative features include a truly open fireplace, open beam work, and a vinyl floor that resembles expensive inlaid Mediterranean tile. The home library is here, as is the music and entertainment center. At right is a desk for going through the day's mail and answering correspondence. Incandescent illumination augments the natural effect of the skylight.

Creating its own sunbelt.
The garden window that's been added changes the whole character of this room. Now, as the sunlight stretches into every corner, whatever the activity that takes place here—reading, playing games, tending the fish in the aquarium—takes on a more lighthearted life. The flooring is a marbleized effect in vinyl-content tile, and this plays off the natural stone of the outside wall.
The light coloring of the floor provides a background for the bright colors of the room and gives the interior a more spacious feeling.

A study in baronial elegance.
The Anglophile in you will react well to this stately family room. The elements that contribute to its palatial look are few but important. Anchoring the scheme are the figures that flank the fireplace. Dark open beams and heavy carved furniture help carry out the atmosphere, as do the armor above the hearth, the deep-set bull's-eye window, and the wall tapestry. The flooring is well-chosen. It looks like expensive brick inset with beams of oak, but actually it's a vinyl flooring in an effect that seems made for such a setting.

Bringing different furniture styles together. Sometimes a small space seems difficult to decorate, mainly because it gives you so little room in which to express yourself. The problem is compounded when you want to include furniture of differing styles. But it is possible to deal with all this attractively. Here the same fabric is used in upholstery and draperies to provide harmony with the variety of other elements in the room, including potted plants, bookshelves, and framed pictures. A Moorish tile effect in embossed linoleum provides a decorative accent.

Mother Nature has her say. With their intriguing colors and textures, natural materials can be given the main role in room decoration. And with results almost as exciting as an African safari, as this room shows. The faux leopard-skin upholstery and zebra rug set the pattern for a scheme that has strong vertical and horizontal lines, as framed by the beams. The fronds of a palm provide a delicate and welcome interruption. The flooring is in a vinyl-content tile effect that suggests the grassy floor of the Serengeti Plain.

Splashes, swatches, and swirls. Lots of color in this room and on the patio adjoining. It's a space intended for young children. But adults also react well to it, because they instantly recognize its practical side. See how extra storage space has been included in an unusual fashion, for example. Note how much natural light floods in from out-of-doors. Above all, look at all the thought that's been given to easy maintenance. Just about every surface can be wiped clean with a damp cloth. That includes the flooring, a vinyl sheet material whose design includes curves that accent and unify the overall room effect.

Opposite:

Say "happiness" with hot colors. A splash of vivid color here and there can be a fine idea. That can spike up the life of a room the way a crowing rooster wakens the dawn. It may not be necessary, though, to keep everything at an nth-degree pitch. For best effect consider using the bright color sparingly, and imbed it in a background that's quieter, more neutral. Here the darkness of the paneling and the furniture and the white vinyl flooring provide backgrounds for the zestful colors and at the same time give unity to the color scheme.

Bring on the toughest kid in the house. Let him do his best. Here's a playroom that's designed to stand up to it, whatever he thinks of. It's planned around a child's activities, and there's lots to do here. The open storage bins, for example, which are intended to encourage him to put toys away at the end of the day, double as a puppet theater. The table and stools wipe clean with a whisk of a sponge, when the inevitable spills occur. The vinyl-content flooring looks expensive but isn't. And with this tile, you could save money by installing it yourself.

Would you install wood planking overhead? Well, you might with *this* planking. It looks like real wood but isn't. It comprises random-width woodgrain boards that a do-it-yourselfer can put up to hide a cracked or stained ceiling. In 1967, when Armstrong advertised this ceiling material, it said that for about $50 you could buy enough of it for a room twelve by fourteen feet in size.

Hiding exposed pipes and wires. In some older homes, the ceilings are exceptionally high. That has certain advantages. The problem is that you sometimes find an unsightly network of plumbing or electrical lines cutting across the room. To this one, the solution is simple: install a suspended ceiling. It hangs in a metal frame that attaches to the old ceiling and provides an attractive overhead surface.

Bring on the activities. Noisy guest-time games or quieter family pursuits. Either way, this room is ready for active living. In the bar area, a row of candles provides a lambent accent to the rough-hewn beams and shingles and to the brick wall surface. The sloped ceiling forms a niche for storing firewood. The flooring, with its custom backgammon inset, is a type of vinyl sheet material with colorfully veined vinyl chips set at random into a translucent vinyl grout. Its texture helps hide scuffs and heel marks, important for a room that invites all sorts of activities.

Comfort me with quiet. A den can double as a place for boisterous family pursuits; but even then, you'd prefer that the noise level be kept under control. One answer is to install an acoustical ceiling. The one in this room is a suspended type. You hang a metal framework from the old ceiling, then drop in the sound-absorbent panels. It's a great way to lower a high ceiling or to hide exposed pipes and wiring. With its louvered shutters and wood-grain paneling, this is now a room to enjoy.

Tile that doesn't look like tile. Those who live in this home decided to enliven the appearance of their den. Already in place was the horizontal paneling of the walls, and they owned a handsome slope-sided desk and bookcase. Now they added perky polka dots at the windows. And they didn't forget the overhead. They installed textured acoustical ceiling tiles with edges so square that they fit together just about seamlessly, to look like an uninterrupted surface.

Worth a lingering look. This home has so many ideas to offer. From the formal dining area in the foreground, your eye moves effortlessly to the family room. From there the glass doors lead to a breezeway. The natural cork wall covering at right harmonizes with the vinyl sheet flooring in a Mediterranean tile effect, and the furniture is chosen to be attractive as well as comfortable. The fireplace wall offers storage space, and the vertical and horizontal lines of the framework add a beautiful proportion to the overall appeal of this space.

Opposite:
When you're bumping into budget restraints. How do you fix up the family room when you really don't have a lot to spend on it? That can be a problem, for sure. One solution is to seek out clever touches that cost little but add a lot of eye-appeal. Note the use of color here, especially the way the red window frames stretch upward in shutter-like extensions that hug the sloped ceiling. The floor covering is an enamel-printed type in a design that resembles a braided rug. Good use is made of vertical paneling and a natural brick texture on the walls.

Natural selection. At times we do well to look to the orderly disparity found in nature to give us direction for decorating. Here the tropical texture of bamboo enlivens the walls, even below the storage-area window seat. The flooring of vinyl-content tile is a good choice for a recreation room because its smooth surface is easy to whisk clean. It uses several colors in a wood-grain effect, installed in a random design that sets off the brightly colored furnishings.

If you want to talk, come in close. This room is spacious enough to accommodate a billiard table, and it even has a cue rack fitted at the end of the bookshelf dividing wall. But it finds room for friendly conversation, too, by clustering twin sofas that face each other. Such a well-lighted corner can give the ordinary family room a whole new set of personalities, because it can be used for a variety of family or guest activities—reading or playing games as well as talking. An area rug helps to tie together the conversation grouping decoratively.

Hunting lodge in the home. Here's a family room with an incontrovertibly masculine air. The flooring of natural cork with a clear vinyl wear layer, inset with black and white vinyl feature strips, leads your eye to the heavy framework of the mantel. Next to it, supported by the storage cupboard at left, is a gun rack. The furniture, sturdy and enduring, is well-chosen to add to the effect; and a color highlight is added by the bright red touches on the walls and in the draperies.

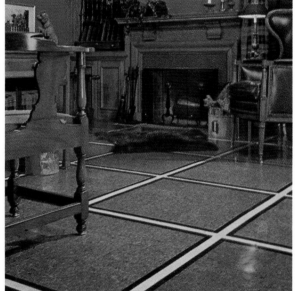

A year-'round room for the family. A playroom for the children, a come-and-relax room for the adults, it's a place in the home that fits the family's activities well, summer and winter. Taupe, mauve, and ivory patterns in the rubber tile floor provide a modest foil for the thick-pile indigo area rug. The flooring and other furnishings were chosen not only for their smart appearance but also for the long service they're expected to provide.

Can Early American exist with contemporary? Yes, and they can get along well together, as this friendly setting suggests. The hearth, the furniture, and the round rug are echoes of Colonial America. And the accessories, including the spice chest and the wrought-iron cabinet hardware, help carry out the theme. But this space was laid out with modern tastes in mind. From anywhere in the family room or the close-by kitchen there's a clear line of sight to the fireplace, which serves as a focal point with its narrow bookshelves on either side. Sliding doors admit plenty of light from the patio outside.

When to use large pattern elements. Plainly designed interiors often benefit from the inclusion of some decorating feature with a dominant attractiveness. Here that function is served by the embossed linoleum in a multi-sized flagstone block design. Though most of the furnishings in the room are neutral in color, they don't lack for style or visual interest. Natural wood-grains, as found in the wall paneling, the valance, and the storage cabinets, offer a warmth that's appealing. And the unusual lighting fixture contrasts nicely with the other furnishings.

Opposite:

No need to opt for the ordinary. Is there a better place to express yourself in interior design than the family room? Probably not, so turn your imagination loose and surprise us. See what's been done here with that offbeat table. It looks like the axe-hewn trunk of a tree, though it's actually the ceramic base for a metallic tray. That's the starting point. Now a note of elegance is added by the darkly mysterious vinyl sheet flooring and by the rich brocade of the upholstery fabric. There! We knew you could do it.

Will you pour? Set up for a tea party for children or an afternoon social for adults, this family room provides an inviting welcome to any guest who enters. Its furniture is comfortable and well-proportioned. The flooring is of vinyl tile in an effect that serves as a textured backdrop for period and contemporary furnishings. This tile comes in one-square-foot blocks, rather than a nine-inch-by-nine-inch size, and that makes for simpler, speedier installation. A potted fern seems to respond to the outdoor greenery seen through the floor-to-ceiling window.

Believe it. This room was decorated on a budget. When financial resources look as if they won't reach quite far enough, that's the time to look for clever decorating ideas that'll stretch those funds like a rubber band. It costs a lot to add a fireplace wall, so in this room a free-standing fireplace fills in nicely. Art reproductions surround it. The banquette along the far wall is made of foot lockers, as is the low table at left. One of the economies came from the tile flooring. It's designed for do-it-yourself installation, and you can save a lot that way.

A do-your-own-thing room. A family room is a ride-your-rocking-horse room, a try-your-hand-at-watercolors room, a write-your-Congressman room, a listen-to-Bach-or-Bacharach room, a curl-up-with-a-good-book room. By definition, it's a space that everybody in the family should find a place in. So when you're designing such a room for your home, it's a good idea to put some of yourself into it. One way to do this, *literally*, is to install the flooring tile yourself (see inset). You can achieve the same fine results shown here. And what a money-saver! The only cost is for the tile and the adhesive. Incidentally, don't miss the stained-glass window effect on either side of the couch.

Chapter 7
Converted "extra-space" rooms

What do you do when you need more space? or when you want to change the function of the space you already have? For example, let's say that your family is growing but your home is not. Or, by contrast, that your sons and daughters have all grown up and left home. Through example, Armstrong shows how to transform an attic storeroom into a boy's bedroom, a breezeway into a family room, an unused basement area into a children's playroom. Here are solutions for any family faced with the problem of needing more room.

If you're adding a room, go about it quietly. Want a model for expanding a house by building an additional room? Here's a good one. The dark wood-grain beams frame the setting, which includes space for the family's collection of antique candle holders, lanterns, and other lighting devices. It's a room intended for television and more active pursuits, and that means a certain amount of racket.

But that's taken care of by the installation of an acoustical ceiling. This one, whose design suggests autumn leaves, complements the colors and fabrics in the room.

This was a garage? Yes, but that was before it saw the light. A growing family sometimes realizes that it needs more space. One solution is to move to a larger house. Another, often more sensible, is to find the room to grow just where you are. Here the garage was the target, and now you step down from the kitchen into an added room that everybody loves. The raised fireplace is new, as are the paneling and the vinyl flooring. Suspending a painting from the handrail balusters is a daring touch that works.

Don't waste a basement. There's no need to, these days, especially if yours is a daylight basement like this. Do a bit of planning, and you can add a usable extra room that the whole family will enjoy. Start by putting down a resilient floor; you can save money if you choose one you can install yourself, such as the vinyl-content tile shown here. When paneling the walls, allow for storage space. Install augmented lighting over any special area, such as a snack table. And you can even set aside one corner of the room for musical programs, if that suits your style.

Opposite, top:
Look around to find extra space. If you wish to expand your home, one way is to add on another room or two. But that may not be necessary if you're able to convert an existing space into a different use. What about the attic or the basement? Could you use the garage or a breezeway? Today's building materials help to make such projects feasible. Here space has been found off the kitchen for a playroom and family room area that includes a breakfast counter. Tan and orange feature strips in the tile floor make the new room appear wider.

Opposite, bottom:
Turn unused space into something admirable. With proper planning, it often is possible to undertake an add-a-room project without busting the budget. In this family room, for example, most of the furnishings are not expensive. The tile flooring, with its chocolate and white feature strips, is a type that can be installed by do-it-yourselfers. Behind the vented fireplace, upholstery fabric is run up the wall to provide a bright accent. Drapes can be drawn to hide a portion of the room when it's not in use.

A trip to the Mediterranean. When the householders who occupy this home transformed their breezeway into a family room, they made two related decisions. First, they wanted to establish a theme for the new area, and they chose the French Riviera as their spot. Second, they wanted to take advantage of the access to the out-of-doors. They turned one corner into a cafe, with a colorful valance setting off a mural. A kiosk adds a festive touch and doubles as storage space. On the patio just outside is an authentic-looking ice cream wagon.

Lost: one garage. Found: one family room. You used to move from the garage into the kitchen. Now you move from the kitchen into a room that every member of the family regards as his or her own. It was a good trade-off. This new family room offers so many possibilities. A pass-through from the kitchen makes it convenient to eat at the breakfast counter, with clearing away the dishes just as easy. The fireplace wall uses the same wall covering as in the kitchen, for decorative unity. And in the corner, the youngsters can entertain with their own puppet shows.

A "suspend story" with a happy ending. An unfinished basement can be the ideal place for a new den or family recreation room. This one features white-painted brick for an interesting textured effect. Don't overlook the shelving. It's simple and inexpensive, but it was done with forethought. It's the right dimension to accommodate those storage bins that add so much color to the room. The suspended acoustical ceiling was easy to install. It hangs in a metal framework from the old ceiling. If you ever have to get to pipes or electrical circuits, just lift out the panels. In a 1967 advertisement, Armstrong said that ceiling materials for this basement den would cost about $75.

Converting a room just for the children? No, not really. It's true that the youngsters of the family tend to drift toward this area, for it offers them so much to do. In addition to (ugh!) homework in the writing-arm chairs at left, they can make music and even stage their own theatrical productions. But adults like this room, too, especially because it's light and cheerful; and as the children grow older and develop new interests, it'll be easy to have the room change with them. There's hardly anything here that can't be readily moved or *removed*.

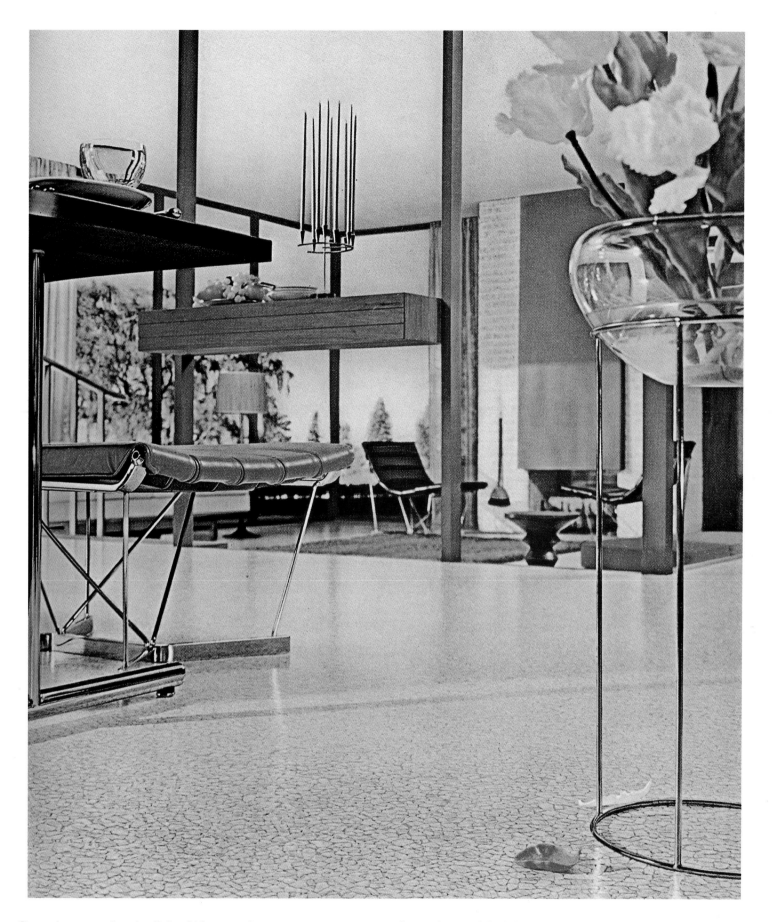

Open it up to the daylight. When you're converting an area of the home into a family room everyone can enjoy, it may be possible to widen its horizons by opening it broadly to the outdoors. This is especially true if it's a breezeway you're converting. Here a window-wall near the fireplace admits plenty of daylight, with all the freshness that implies. In an unusual vase stand in the right foreground, cut flowers offset the sheer vertical and horizontal lines of the new setting. Chrome, leather, and natural wood-grains predominate in the furnishings.

Can you see the aurora borealis from here? When the people who live here converted attic space into a new family room, they wanted, first, to expand their interest in astronomy and, second, to reflect their Finnish heritage. Didn't they accomplish both very well, though? Rustic simplicity, clean lines, and a natural look are characteristic of decoration from Finland. The low furniture, the indirect lighting, and the geometric angles of the beamed ceiling all contribute to the effect. Storage space is plentiful along the paneled walls.

The taste of a villa in Tangier. The intricate screens that border this room show that its inspiration came from across the sea. The appeal of Moroccan design lies in its intriguing detail, graceful patterns, and rich textures. The Alhambresque ornamentation is picked up in the lighting fixture that hangs over the couch, in the pierced-metal lantern over the desk at right, and in the heavily carved furniture. The surfeit of cushions tells us that this is a place to relax. And if you're converting a room in your home, here's one way to do it with great style!

All set up for bridge. If you're converting space into a family room, keep in mind that you'll want to use it for entertaining guests, too. Here's a room that's designed with company in mind. The period furniture is stylish and pleasant, and guests aren't likely ever to tire of it. At right an old chest, with its heavily ornamented hardware, is a handy storage place for games and other items that tend to clutter a room that's used constantly. Near the ceiling a plate rail holds treasured porcelain pieces, which lead your eye to the well-tailored garden just outside.

This corral is plenty OK. As the family grows, it may be possible to let the house grow along with it. Add a room like this one, and don't be surprised to find that the youngsters take it over fast. That's all right, because they need a place to play—and besides, it's about as childproof as any room can be. The flooring is a durable vinyl-content tile in a styling that resembles real mosaic, and inset feature strips add color. Young cowboys and cowgirls (see inset) enjoy playing within the fenced-in corral, which has its own fantasy saguaro cactus. Head 'em up!

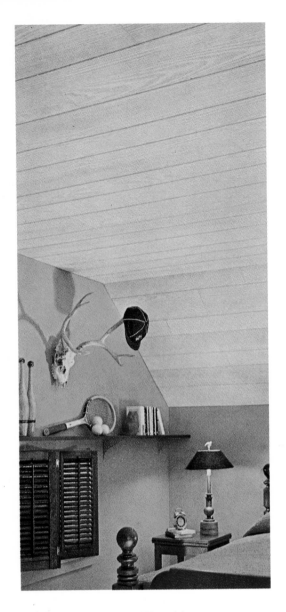

Right:

A game room fits into the basement. The basement may be the first place to look if you want to expand your home by adding an extra-purpose room. One problem often comes up, though: what do you do about those overhead floor joists, with the pipes and wiring running through them? The solution is a suspended ceiling. Hang a metal grid by wires from above, then drop in the noise-reducing ceiling panels. In 1968 Armstrong said that for a room twelve by fourteen feet in size all the materials for a ceiling like this would cost about $65.

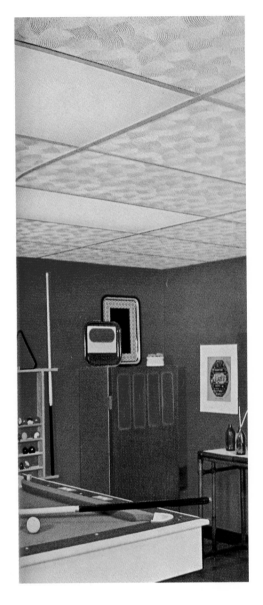

An attic hideaway. The older son of the family was of an age at which he deserved a place of his own. But there was no room available. Yes, there was! It took a bit of imagination to see that unused space in the attic could be transformed into something special. Now look at the result. He has room for the tools of his own interests. Shutters at the window lessen the light when that's desirable. And the ceiling, of a type that the family members could install themselves, is of random-width boards with a graining that looks like real wood but isn't.

Don't forget to include storage space. In a daylight basement, an unused area of the home can be put to multiple purposes. In this home such space has become a family center, with a corner set aside as an office with its own telephone. In planning such an added room, you never go wrong by making allowance for storage. Look for unusual places to tuck it in, as was done here in the lower part of the banquette that lines the window. Sunlight streaming through the shelves shows off gleaming glassware collectibles.

Opposite page, bottom:
Do-it-yourself design. Flooring tiles in a sea of styling effects and pattern colors are made for installation by the home handyman or -woman. That's worth keeping in mind when you're planning the conversion of attic or basement space into a new room for your home, because it can mean a substantial cost saving. But at the same time, remember the design possibilities in tile installation. The tiles are laid one at a time, so they can form an almost limitless variety of designs. In this basement, the eye-catching resilient tile floor gives the area a furnished feeling and at the same time offers a colorful decorative touch to the interior. Of course this same flooring effect could be carried out in a number of color combinations.

Hard to believe how little this one cost. In the 1960s Armstrong undertook a project: assuming the homeowners were willing to do the work themselves, how could they turn a basement into a family recreation room for minimum cost? Here's the result. Do-it-yourself installations of vinyl-content flooring tile and an acoustical ceiling were the starting points. The high basement windows are still there, but now they're disguised to look like full-length windows by the striped curtains that reach all the way to the floor. Those curtains are flanked by panels of fiberboard, painted dull black to contrast with the white-painted concrete block walls. The furniture was moved in from the patio, because it's not needed out there except during warmer weather. Aren't those paintings colorful? They're posters of foreign lands, obtained from travel agencies. Back then, the total cost of materials for this room conversion, including flooring tile, ceiling material, and lighting fixtures, was less than $300!

Opposite:
Open the door to a golden age. Class all the way. That's what this entryway suggests. The moment you come into the home, your eye moves to the specially designed brass sunburst in the floor. It's set into vinyl flooring that shimmers with golden tracery, transforming the classic beauty of marble into lavish modern elegance. The draperies are hung in a way that allows the windows to echo the trim above the doorway. Even the stairway is richly ornamented with brass, helping to maintain consistency in the overall decorating scheme.

Chapter 8
Entryways, offices, and other rooms

In this chapter are assembled the rooms that somehow don't fit easy classification—the home office, the apartment, the solarium, the music room. Each one offers decorative ideas that could be adapted for other areas of the home. Note especially the change that occurs in the entryway as it becomes more spacious, more open, more an imposing contributor to the first impression you form as you come into the home. Oh, by the way. Don't overlook the pleasures of living in a lighthouse. That's shown here, too!

You could raise your own orchids. You could do a lot of interesting things with a solarium like this in your home. It's a natural place for luxuriant greenery, of course. But with those high-back wicker chairs, can't you also see it as a setting for sunlit afternoon entertaining? A room like this one calls for an especially attractive floor, one that's easy to maintain. This flooring is a sheet vinyl type, with tiny squares of vinyl set into a translucent vinyl grout so they look like Mediterranean tesserae. And any spills clean up readily with the swish of a damp mop.

The enduring character of good taste. Everything about this home office and library says quality and timeless appeal. Note the subtle simplicity of the fireplace wall, for example, and how it becomes the focal point of the room. The furniture is stable and comfortable, with styling unlikely ever to look dated. Lighting levels are purposely kept muted, except at the desk and in reading areas where stronger illumination is appropriate. An area rug covers a portion of the vinyl flooring, which has contrasting inlays to give the room further dimension.

An entryway as light and airy as the rest of the home. In many a home, the main entrance is dark and discouraging—not intentionally, but just because little thought was given to its planning. That's too bad, because this "first impression" area can be made as open and inviting as any other room. Here a floor-to-ceiling window, with leafy plants just outside, welcomes sunshine and guests alike. A large mirror reflects the scene, as always giving the illusion of greater space. The draperies in the dining room have the same pattern as the wallpaper in the entryway.

154

What do you call a room with so many functions? The kids think of it as their playroom, the adults as a television room. It's a room for entertaining guests, too, even dinner guests. Well, a *multipurpose* room is what it is, because it accommodates so many activities. The attractive shutters that close off the lower portion of the windows are repeated in those that fold over the television set when it's not in use. Storage cabinets that flank the banquette double as end tables. Additional storage is available in the divider wall at left.

Right now it's a party place. Usually this is a dining nook. But as quickly as you can sing "Happy birthday to you," it can be transformed into a special place for a party. The scroll-work chairs give it the feel of an old-fashioned ice cream parlor. The vinyl flooring is especially appropriate for this kind of room. Spills wipe up readily from its surface, and it offers a festive decorative elegance, too. In 1961 advertising, Armstrong said that for a room twelve by fifteen feet in size this flooring would cost about $195, including installation.

An exclamation of sunlight to greet you. In an entryway, or anywhere in the home that you wish to dramatize with a catch-your-breath accent, consider a stylized sunburst like this. It points the way to other decorative elements that shouldn't be ignored, such as the carved furniture, the richly ornamented cupboard that's built into the wall, and even the tastefully set bookshelves. The graceful fronds of a fern contrast with the straight lines of the sunburst, which is set into a vinyl sheet flooring that scatters chips of color at random across its surface.

Home office for a business traveler. When your business or profession takes you on the road—and you know there'll be details to take care of when you get back home—it has to be a comfort to know that waiting to welcome you is a room like this one. It's well-equipped, well-lighted, and well-suited for work. Furthermore, the comfortable couches at left can be used as beds, so the space doubles as a guest room when needed. It even has a sunken fireplace. An area rug is laid over the vinyl sheet flooring, which features pebble-like chips set into a clear grout.

Which decorative treatment do you prefer? Here's the same residential entryway, handled two different ways. And what a dramatic change! In the treatment at left, the furniture is provincial and graceful. Above, it's massive and more masculine. Probably the most important difference is that seen in the choice of floors. At left is a blending of vinyl tiles, including one type with a paisley design. Above, inset with white vinyl stars, is a cork tile with a clear vinyl surface. Each of these interiors has its own striking appeal. Your choice!

Suggested by a villa in Sicily. Deep, rich color and intricate design are the essence of Sicilian decorating, and this entrance hall captures its Mediterranean ancestry in a spirited way. Everywhere is beauty, with the ornate carving of the door reflected in the shelf bracket, the window seat, and even the stairway. Sunlight shooting through the lozenge panels of the window creates an interesting, changing pattern across the walls and floor. An area rug in an unusual shape provides a decorative accent, as does the imported tall-case clock next to the door.

All day long, this room stays busy. The front hall. Hardly any area in the house sees more people flowing through it, friends and family members alike. In your home, it's the opening act. Look at all the practical ideas this one offers. Beneath a bright, welcoming painting is a handy shelf for your guests to use. Tall windows invite the sunlight to come in. But stormy days have been considered, too. The guest closet has vented doors, convenient for airing wet rain gear. The flooring has the natural look of slate; but actually it's vinyl, so it's a snap to maintain.

An illusion in color. This intriguing entryway features a custom flooring inset in which the colors appear to overlap. They don't. It's all an illusion, made possible through the clever combination of six of the pattern colors available within one type of sheet vinyl flooring. Here, the painting on the far wall provided the inspiration. But such is the variety of styles and colors available in resilient flooring that today's home can draw on a wide variety of idea-stimulating themes in much the same way and turn them into decorative masterpieces.

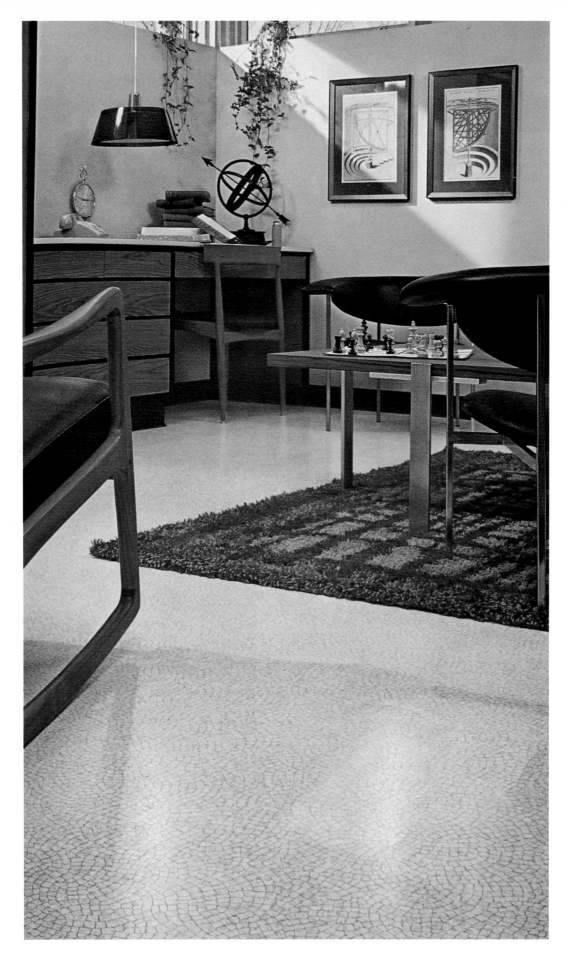

All work and no play. Well, at least a *little* play, because this home office includes an area that can be used as a quiet game room, study, or family den. The space is warm, inviting, and memorable. From the leather-seated rocker at left to the desk chair to the chairs around the table, the furnishings are coordinated and contemporary. A hanging fixture spills light onto the desk, augmenting the sunlight that flares in through the high windows. A pair of potted plants, dangling their tendrils along the wall, break up the straight-line formality of the room.

Come into a fortune. Well, it *looks* like a fortune, at any rate. The moment you step into this richly appointed home, you know you're in the presence of good taste. The graceful sweep of the stairway, the gentle arc of the fanlight over the entry door, the well-chosen furnishings, all speak of unques-tionable elegance. But don't get the idea that practicality is ignored. See that floor? It's an especially durable vinyl sheet material, intended to hold its beauty through the years. Its design features stone-like vinyl chips and a rich, distinctive texture.

This way to the music room. Open design leads to intriguing possibilities in decoration. As you come into this home through the main entryway, you pass a desk on your way to an area set aside for music. At left, shrubs and saplings offer their natural foliage as a contrast to the sheer, straight lines of the wooden beamwork. Choose the floor with care, because it's usually the largest decorating element in a room. Here the choice was Spanish tile. Wait a minute! That just *looks* like Spanish tile. Actually, it's vinyl, and that means simple maintenance.

Come in out of the rain. An entry hall is often the favorite trackin'-in room in the house, and its floor has to be able to withstand the worst that the natural elements can throw at it on a dingy day. Vinyl sheet flooring was a good choice here, as its Mediterranean tile design can stay bright and cheerful with an occasional swish of a damp mop. It's not the only clever idea here, though. See that twin-partition divider? It hides a closet for your rain-wet slickers. At its foot, an attractive pebbled area makes a great place for drying umbrellas and boots.

168

Does this look like just another floor? Years ago, the floor was just something underfoot. Something to be ignored, to be decorated around. Then designers came to realize that the floor is usually the largest decorating element in a room, and it shouldn't be overlooked. Moreover, it opens up unusually fine possibilities in interior design, especially because of today's panoply of floor styles. In this entryway, for example, the basic theme is simple, classic, and unadorned. But the flooring, a vinyl-content tile, gives a dramatic flourish to the effect.

Penthouse apartment with a view, inside and out.
Here's an interior capable of competing with the sunset-silhouetted skyline. The furnishings offer excitement in shapes, fabrics, and colors. A dashing swipe of scarlet around the windows is answered in the carpet. Wet-look upholstery fabric envelops the sofa and chair right down to the squared-off legs, and the seat cushions slide into the curved arms to create a graceful, clean look. The brilliantly lacquered table, with its glass top, provides a central accent to the apartment.

Brighten the corner. A family den doesn't have to be dour and drear. In this one, pastels in the walls and upholstery establish the dominant color. But daylight is always welcome, and here it pushes through the deep-set window and through the leaves of a hanging plant. Now look up. The cool coloration and delicate pattern of the ceiling tile actually become part of the room's decorative scheme. It's an acoustical ceiling, so it can make the home quieter and more comfortable, helping to diffuse the noise of television set, electric appliance, or children's play.

Give an apartment the patina of a showplace. You're going to turn a small area of your home into a mother-in-law's apartment. With a small extra push, you can turn it into a space that everybody can be proud of. This one has built-in bookshelves, comfortable furniture, and sunlight that dapples its way through a large fern. The flooring makes it extra-special. It's a natural cork tile with a clear vinyl wear layer, and it glows with a lustrous tortoise-shell look.

Making a small space pull its weight. When you're working in confined quarters, as in this entryway, don't be afraid to plunge into the fray with forceful design elements. Here two patterns of a vinyl tile create a strong statement in the flooring. The unmistakable verticality of the wallpaper stripes, the shirred curtains, and the harmonizing colors of the closet doors chip in their own contribution. And, as is often the case in a small area, a mirror helps to make the room look larger.

An impression that stays in the memory. Here's a library setting that's hard to forget, for several reasons. The long stretch of couch leads to the corner, then bends around it. Wood-grain wall paneling is reflected in the beams that frame the windows. The natural beauty of cork in the flooring tile is sealed under a wear layer of clear vinyl, for added durability and easier maintenance. Add shelves for books, a glittering chandelier, and intricate wood carvings, and you have a room that's beautifully established for reading and quiet conversation.

Elegance edged with restraint. The moment you step in, you know that you're in the presence of something special: an exquisite aura of formality, yet one that glows with a feeling of warmth and ease, and with a touch of the Welch. From the chandelier that leads your eye to the living room at left to the gracefully arched entry to the library at right, the home's balance and proportion resound with good taste. Lightly indented molding helps to carry out the theme, even in the wall area surrounding the portrait. The flooring is in two colorings of a vinyl sheet material, with copper inset.

Could you live in a lighthouse? Let's imagine that you're an amateur bassoonist and that your spouse likes to do blacksmithing at home. You're eager to settle into well-deserved (and, by your neighbors, much-appreciated) solitude. If you're fortunate, you could find a place like this: brass banisters, stairs to climb for day-in, day-out fitness, and an unobstructed view of 7,000 square miles of the Atlantic. Living beside the sea, you'll be grateful for the flooring that covers the stairsteps. It's a durable vinyl sheet flooring, and tracked-in sand sweeps right off its surface. By the way, this home offers *plenty* of illumination!

Notes